# A Brief
# Catechism
# For Adults

THIS BOOKS BELONGS TO:

Name _____

Street _____

City _____ State _____ Zip _____

## WHO IS TAKING INSTRUCTIONS AT

Name of Church: _____

Street _____

City _____ State _____ Zip _____

Instructions are given on _____
_(days of the week)_

at _____
_(time of instructions)_

Hours of Masses on Sunday morning:

Priest's Telephone Number: _____

# A Brief Catechism For Adults

## A Complete Handbook On How To Be A Good Catholic

By
Fr. William J. Cogan

*"From thy youth up receive instruction, and even to thy grey hairs thou shalt find wisdom. Come to her as one that plougheth, and soweth, and wait for her good fruits: For in working about her thou shalt labour a little, and shalt quickly eat of her fruits."*

—Ecclesiasticus 6:18-20

TAN BOOKS AND PUBLISHERS, INC.
Rockford, Illinois 61105

Nihil Obstat:      Joseph Egan, S.J.

Imprimatur:      ✠ Samuel Cardinal Stritch
                 Archbishop of Chicago
                 May 25, 1958

Published in 1958 under the title *A Catechism for Adults* by ACTA (Adult Catechetical Teaching Aids) Foundation, Chicago, a not-for-profit foundation under the supervision of the Archbishop of Chicago.

ISBN: 0-89555-492-5

Library of Congress Catalog Card No.: 93-60780

Printed and bound in the United States of America.

TAN BOOKS AND PUBLISHERS, INC.
P.O. Box 424
Rockford, Illinois 61105
1993

*"God, who at sundry times and in divers manners spoke in times past to the fathers by the prophets, last of all in these days hath spoken to us by his Son, whom he hath appointed heir of all things, by whom also he made the world."*

—Hebrews 1:1

# Publisher's Note

This edition of *A Brief Catechism for Adults*—the classic textbook for converts by the late Fr. William J. Cogan, a priest of the archdiocese of Chicago, now currently published by TAN Books and Publishers, Inc.—has been carefully revised and enlarged to reflect certain disciplinary changes that have been made in the Catholic Church (e.g., changes in fasting regulations), while at the same time to indicate as well the traditional norms that were in effect when the author wrote the book.

Virtually the entire original text of the book is intact in this edition, plus a few supplementary questions and answers have been included. Next, a few extra paragraphs have been added here and there to the "Practical Points" at the end of some chapters. Also, all Bible quotes have been changed to the Douay-Rheims version for the additional authority and power which this classic Catholic version of the Bible renders, as does none other. And finally, the entire book has been retypeset in a larger, more legible face, that nonetheless still looks exactly like the original and that follows the original in style and format to the letter.

The final result has been carefully checked for doctrinal accuracy and we believe would receive the hearty endorsement of the author as a generally much improved edition of his already brilliantly conceived and beautifully executed *A Catechism for Adults.*

There is really no other short adult catechism quite like it for convert instruction and Catholic adult review. It is, therefore, the sincere hope of the publishers that this book will enjoy wide use by priests instructing prospective Catholics, as well as by Catholics already within the Fold.

—Thomas A. Nelson
August 11, 1993
Feast of St. Philomena

# Contents

# CONTENTS

# Author's Preface

This book is the work of many priests who actually instruct prospective converts from all walks of life. The original mimeographed edition was based on the series of instructions given by priests engaged in convert work for many years in the Archdiocese of Chicago. After being used experimentally for several inquiry classes, it was revised according to the suggestions of these priests. Since its first edition in 1951, it has become practically the standard catechism for instructing non-Catholics, not only in the United States and Canada, but wherever English is spoken. Priests from all over the world have sent their suggestions and comments for making the catechism even better. The author appreciates their help and hopes that they and the other priests who use this book will continue with their suggestions.

Special thanks are due Father Edward B. Brueggeman, S.J., S.T.D. and Father William A. Dowd, S.J., M.A., S.T.D., S.S.L. of St. Mary of the Lake Seminary; Father Edward Dufficy, M.A., S.T.B., of Quigley Seminary; Father George A. Herdegen, M.A., S.T.L., J.C.L. of the Matrimonial Tribunal of the Archdiocese of Chicago; Father Walter Imbiorski, M.A., S.T.L. of the Cana Conference; Father Elmer Wurth, M.M. of the Maryknoll Seminary in Glen Ellen, Illinois; Fathers Henry J. Pehler, M.A., S.T.L., Francis McGrath, M.A., S.T.B., Robert E. Burns, M.A., S.T.L. and Howard Tuite, M.A., S.T.L. parish priests of the Archdiocese of Chicago; all of whom worked very hard with the author in preparing this revision.

This edition, while following the time-tried, traditional approach to the Catholic religion, has incorporated what is good in newer techniques. The more abundant use of Holy Scripture, the "Practical Points" at the end of each lesson and the shorter answers will be welcomed by the priests who use this catechism.

This book aims at three things:

**1st, Clearness** in teaching religion so that the prospective convert can clearly know what he is supposed to believe and do in order to save his soul. The book is not meant to be a theological manual, but rather a handbook in which non-Catholics can find the main ideas given in the instructions.

**2nd, Ordinary language.** The book has been written in the language spoken by people of today. The use of theological terms and anglicized Latin words has been avoided as much as possible. Actual experience in giving the final examination to thousands of non-Catholics has helped the author to express theological concepts in the familiar words of everyday conversation.

**3rd, Correct emphasis** on the things necessary to form a Christian conscience. The book is designed to prepare its users for conversion, not to make theologians of them. Hence the author has tried to give the proper emphasis to sin, Heaven, Hell, prayer, the necessity of grace and the Sacraments. The special treatment of Marriage and family life is based on the conviction that most people will save their souls or lose them as married people, and that, therefore, they should clearly know their duties as married people and as parents.

It is hoped that this book will help priests in leading to the Master those who until now have had only a few crumbs that fell from His table.

—Rev. William J. Cogan
1958

# Introduction

For many people, God is some kind of vague Power who exists somewhere in outer space and who somehow created the world but who is not interested in the people who live on this planet. Nothing could be further from the truth. In studying these lessons, you will see how really interested God is in you and how much He loves you. The instructions which you will receive from the priest will make you more aware of God's love for you. You will also realize how much you have missed in life, and later on you will thank God for bringing you to take the instructions. This is, indeed, a demonstration of His great love for you.

# $\mathcal{L}$ε**ss**on 1: Religion

## 1. What is the purpose of these lessons?

To fill in what is missing in the lives of so many people—the knowledge and practice of true religion.

*"The heart of the wise seeketh instruction: and the mouth of fools feedeth on foolishness."* (Proverbs 15:14).

## 2. Why is religion the most important study you can take up?

Because God expects you to know what He has taught and what He wants you to do in this life.

*"Let no man deceive himself: if any man among you seem to be wise in this world, let him become a fool, that he may be wise. For the wisdom of this world is foolishness with God."* (1 Corinthians 3:18-19).

## 3. What is religion?

Religion consists of two parts:

1) Believing everything God has told the human race.

2) Observing all your duties to God, yourself and your fellow men.

*"Be ye doers of the word, and not hearers only, deceiving your own selves."* (James 1:22).

## 4. Is religion really necessary?

Yes, for several reasons—

1) God demands that every human being follow His plan of life.

2) Without religion, life is meaningless.

3) Lack of religion causes unhappiness, both in this life and in the next.

*"For he that rejecteth wisdom, and discipline, is unhappy: and their hope is vain, and their labours without fruit, and their works unprofitable. Their wives are foolish, and their children wicked."* (Wisdom 3:11-12).

1

**5. What will happen to those who do not practice religion?**

They will be punished with the everlasting torments of Hell.

*"The Lord Jesus shall be revealed from heaven, with the angels of his power: in a flame of fire, giving vengeance to them who know not God, and who obey not the gospel of our Lord Jesus Christ."* (2 Thessalonians 1:7-8).

**6. What will religion give you in this life?**

Peace of mind, which is greater than anything money can buy.

*"Blessed are they who hear the word of God, and keep it."* (Luke 11:28). *"Much peace have they that love thy law, and to them there is no stumbling block."* (Psalm 118:165).

**7. Are all religions the same?**

No, there is only one true religion, the one established by God Himself, which is explained in this book.

# $\mathcal{L}$ε44οn 2:  The Bible and Tradition

*"God, who at sundry times and in divers manners spoke in times past to the fathers by the prophets, last of all in these days hath spoken to us by his Son, whom he hath appointed heir of all things, by whom also he made the world."* (Hebrews 1:1).

**1. What is the Bible?**

A collection of the writings which were inspired by God.

> *"All scripture, inspired of God, is profitable to teach, to reprove, to correct, to instruct in justice, that the man of God may be perfect, furnished to every good work."* (2 Timothy 3:16-17).

**2. What does "inspired by God" mean?**

It means that God chose some men and moved them to write down faithfully all the things, and only those things, which He wanted written down.

> *"For prophecy came not by the will of man at any time: but the holy men of God spoke, inspired by the Holy Ghost."* (2 Peter 1:21).

**3. Who, then, is the primary author of the Bible?**

God is, since He moved these men to write down the things He ordered, although He allowed them to write in their own language and style.

> *"For I give you to understand, brethren, that the gospel which was preached by me is not according to man. For neither did I receive it of man, nor did I learn it; but by the revelation of Jesus Christ."* (Galatians 1:11-12).

**4. How many writings, or books, are there in the Bible?**

There are 72.

**5. When were all these writings put together?**

The Catholic Church put all of them into one book between the years 350 and 405.

3

## 6. How is the Bible divided?

It is divided into two main parts, the Old Testament and the New Testament.

*The Old Testament contains the things God told the human race from the beginning of the world up to the coming of His Son, Jesus Christ. The New Testament contains what God has told us through His Son and through His Apostles and others.*

## 7. Is it possible to misunderstand the Bible?

Yes, even the Bible itself says so.

*"As also in all his [St. Paul's] epistles, speaking in them of these things; in which are certain things hard to be understood, which the unlearned and unstable wrest [twist], as they do also the other scriptures, to their own destruction."* (2 Peter 3:16).

## 8. How can you get the true meaning of the Bible?

You can get it only from God's official interpreter, the Catholic Church.

*"Understanding this first, that no prophecy of scripture is made by private interpretation."* (2 Peter 1:20).

## 9. Is everything that God taught in the Bible?

No, the rest is in Tradition.

*"Many other signs also did Jesus in the sight of his disciples, which are not written in this book."* (John 20:30).

## 10. What is Tradition?

The Unwritten Word of God: these "other things Jesus did" were handed down by word of mouth by the Apostles and other close followers of Jesus.

*"Therefore, brethren, stand fast; and hold the traditions which you have learned, whether by word, or by our epistle."* (2 Thessalonians 2:14).

## 11. Do you have to believe in Tradition?

Yes, because it is the Word of God and has equal authority with the Bible.

*The early Christians learned everything by Tradition, since only later on were some of the teachings of Jesus written down, the last writing being done at the end of the first century. That is, there was no New Testament in the early Church.*

## 12. Are you free to believe whatever you want?

No, you have to believe everything in the Bible and Tradition—all the doctrines which the Catholic Church teaches.

*"The Lord Jesus shall be revealed from heaven, with the angels of his power: in a flame of fire, giving vengeance to them who know not God, and who obey not the gospel of our Lord Jesus Christ."* (2 Thessalonians 1:7-8).

## 13. What kind of sin is it to deny anything the Catholic Church teaches?

Usually it is a serious sin, that is, a mortal sin.

*"Whosoever revolteth, and continueth not in the doctrine of Christ, hath not God. He that continueth in the doctrine, the same hath both the Father and the Son."* (2 John 1:9).

## PRACTICAL POINTS

1. If a Catholic denies one or more of the doctrines of the Catholic Church, he is no longer a Catholic. To be a Catholic is to accept the Catholic faith in its entirety because it comes from God, and God can neither lie nor make a mistake.

2. There can be no contradiction between the Bible and science since both are concerned with unchangeable Truth. For example, the "six days" in the creation account may well have been intended symbolically rather than literally.

3. You can easily tell the difference between a Catholic Bible and a non-Catholic one. A Catholic Bible always has the name of a Catholic bishop near the front with the Latin word *Imprimatur,* which means "It may be printed."

4. The Catholic Church not only allows her members to read the Bible, but encourages them to do so. She gives special "blessings" (called indulgences) to those who read it as spiritual reading. You are encouraged to buy a Catholic Bible and read part of it every day.

5

5. Protestant Bibles are missing 7 books of the Bible. Martin Luther, the founder of Protestantism, decided to omit them because the Jews omit them. Catholics call these 7 books the "Deuterocanonical Books"; Protestants call them the "Apocrypha." They are *Tobias, Judith, Wisdom, Ecclesiasticus, Baruch,* and *1* and *2 Machabees* (plus parts of *Esther* and *Daniel*).

6. Nowhere does the Bible say that the Bible is the sole source of Christian teaching. This fact refutes the classic Protestant teaching of "the Bible alone" *(sola Scriptura)*.

# $\mathcal{L}$esson 3: God and The Holy Trinity

*"Oh, the depth of the riches of the wisdom and of the knowledge of God! How incomprehensible are his judgments and how unsearchable his ways! For who hath known the mind of the Lord, or who hath been his counsellor? Or who hath first given to him, and recompense shall be made him? For of him and by him and in him, are all things: to him be glory for ever. Amen."* (Romans 11:33-36).

### 1. Who Is God?

God is the Supreme Being, the Creator "who made heaven and earth, the sea, and all things that are in them." (Psalm 145:5).

### 2. What does "Creator" mean?

It means that God made all things out of nothing.

*"I beseech thee, my son, look upon heaven and earth, and all that is in them: and consider that God made them out of nothing, and mankind also."* (2 Machabees 7:28).

### 3. What is a creature?

A creature is anything made by God.

### 4. How do you know there is a God?

If you just examine the things in this world, you have to admit that someone had to make them.

*"But ask now the beasts, and they shall teach thee: and the birds of the air, and they shall tell thee. Speak to the earth, and it shall answer thee: and the fishes of the sea shall tell. Who is ignorant that the hand of the Lord hath made all these things?"* (Job 12:7-9).
*"The fool hath said in his heart: There is no God."* (Psalm 13:1).

### 5. Why can you not see God?

Because He has no body.

*"God is a spirit."* (John 4:24).

## 6. Where is God?

God is everywhere.

*"Whither shall I go from thy spirit? or whither shall I flee from thy face? If I ascend into heaven, thou art there: if I descend into hell, thou art present."* (Psalm 138:7-8).

## 7. Can God see all things?

Yes, because He is everywhere.

*"The eyes of the Lord in every place behold the good and the evil."* (Proverbs 15:3).

## 8. How old is God?

God is ageless, eternal, which means that He had no beginning and will have no end and will never change.

*"Before the mountains were made, or the earth and the world was formed; from eternity and to eternity thou art God."* (Psalm 89:2).

## 9. Can God do all things?

Yes, "With God all things are possible." (Matthew 19:26).

## 10. Is God alive?

Yes, He is alive and is the source of all life.

*Over 30 Bible references call Him "the living God." "All things were made by him: and without him was made nothing that was made. In him was life."* (John 1:3-4).

## 11. Is God independent and unlimited?

Yes, He depends on nothing and is unlimited (infinite) in every way.

*"Neither is he served with men's hands, as though he needed any thing; seeing it is he who giveth to all life, and breath, and all things."* (Acts 17:25).

## 12. Is God interested in you?

Yes, and He loves you with an unlimited love.

*"Can a woman forget her infant, so as not to have pity on the son of her womb? and if she should forget, yet will not I forget thee."* (Isaias 49:15).

### 13. Will God forgive you your sins?

Yes, if you are truly sorry for them.

*"For the Lord your God is merciful, and will not turn away his face from you, if you return to him."* (2 Paralipomenon 30:9).

### 14. What is the Holy Trinity?

This means that there are three Persons in One God.

*"Going therefore, teach ye all nations; baptizing them in the name of the Father, and of the Son, and of the Holy Ghost."* (Matthew 28:19).

### 15. Who are the three Persons in God?

God the Father, God the Son and God the Holy Ghost.

*"And there are three who give testimony in heaven, the Father, the Word, and the Holy Ghost. And these three are one."* (1 John 5:7).

### 16. Are the three Persons of the Holy Trinity equal?

Yes, they are equal to One Another, but each One is a separate and distinct Person, and each One is God.

### 17. How can there be three persons in only one God?

This is a mystery that no human mind can completely understand.

## PRACTICAL POINTS

1. There are many things in this world which the human mind cannot understand, such as growth, sight, hearing, electricity. Therefore, we should not be surprised to find that we cannot completely understand the God who made the world.

2. Faith is accepting something on the word of another. God says there are three Persons in the One God. If you accept that statement as being true because He said so, then you have faith.

3. Faith is not unreasonable if what you are told is possible and if the person telling you is usually truthful and has nothing to gain from telling you a lie.

**4.** Human beings can tell lies, but God cannot because He is Truth Itself. Therefore, believing anything God says is the highest kind of faith. This kind of faith, however, is a gift that you must pray for.

# ℒℯ𝓈𝓈ℴ𝓃 4:  Prayer

*"Ask, and it shall be given you: seek, and you shall find: knock, and it shall be opened to you. For every one that asketh, receiveth: and he that seeketh, findeth: and to him that knocketh, it shall be opened. Or what man is there among you, of whom if his son shall ask bread, will he reach him a stone? Or if he shall ask him a fish, will he reach him a serpent? If you then being evil, know how to give good gifts to your children: how much more will your Father who is in heaven, give good things to them that ask him?"* (Matthew 7:7-11).

### 1. What is prayer?

Prayer is the raising of the mind and heart to God.

### 2. Why should you pray?

You should pray—

1) to adore God, to tell Him that He made you and that you depend upon Him for absolutely everything.

2) to thank God for the blessings He has given you.

> *"What hast thou that thou hast not received? And if thou hast received, why dost thou glory, as if thou hadst not received it?"* (1 Corinthians 4:7).

3) to ask God's pardon for your sins.

> *"O God, be merciful to me a sinner."* (Luke 18:13).

4) to ask God's help in all things.

> *"Ask, and it shall be given you: seek, and you shall find: knock, and it shall be opened to you."* (Matthew 7:7).

### 3. When should you pray?

Every day, especially—

1) in the morning—to offer the day to God and to ask for His help in the temptations of the day.

11

2) during the day, especially during temptations.

3) at night—to thank God for the blessings of the day and to ask Him to forgive you for the sins committed that day.

4) before and after meals.

*The prayers to be said every day are on Pages 161 and 162.*

## 4. To whom should you pray?

1) To God the Father, God the Son and God the Holy Ghost.

2) You may also pray to the Blessed Virgin, the Angels and the Saints.

*"And the smoke of the incense of the prayers of the saints ascended up before God from the hand of the angel."* (Apocalypse 8:4).

## 5. Why may you pray to the Blessed Virgin, the Angels and the Saints?

Because they are God's best friends; God will listen to them more than to us who are still sinners.

*"Go to my servant Job, and offer for yourselves a holocaust: and my servant Job shall pray for you: his face I will accept, that folly be not imputed to you: for you have not spoken right things before me, as my servant Job hath."* (Job 42:8).

## 6. For whom should you pray?

1) For everyone still on earth, even your enemies.

*"But I say to you, love your enemies: do good to them who hate you: and pray for them that persecute and calumniate you."* (Matthew 5:44).

2) For the souls in Purgatory. (See Lesson 12.)

## 7. What should you pray for?

Every day pray to get into Heaven; when praying for anything else, always say, "If it is Thy will, Lord."

*"For after all these things do the heathens seek. For your Father knoweth that you have need of all these things. Seek ye therefore first the kingdom of God, and his justice, and all these things shall be added unto you."* (Matthew 6:32-33).

**8. Does God always hear your prayers?**

Yes, but He does not always give what you ask for, because you sometimes ask for things that are bad for you, or you do not ask God properly.

**9. Does God hear (i.e., answer) the prayers of sinners who are living in mortal sin?**

He hears their prayers for the grace of true repentance, but He does not hear their prayers for other favors, unless they are willing to give up their sins and do penance.

*"Now we know that God doth not hear sinners: but if a man be a server of God, and doth his will, him he heareth."* (John 9:31).

**10. Should only good people pray?**

No, everyone should pray. Especially should mortal sinners pray to be delivered from their sins.

*"I desire not the [eternal] death of the wicked, but that the wicked turn from his way, and live."* (Ezechiel 33:11). *"For every one that asketh, receiveth."* (Matthew 7:8).

**11. How should you pray?**

1) With *attention*, keeping your mind on your prayer.

2) With *humility*, realizing that you are powerless without God.

3) With *confidence*, realizing that God can do all things.

4) With *perseverance*, without giving up hope.

*"And this is the confidence which we have towards him: That, whatsoever we shall ask according to his will, he heareth us."* (1 John 5:14).

**12. Why is public prayer necessary?**

Because, as members of human society, we owe God public recognition of Him as Supreme Master of society.

**13. How does public prayer help the world?**

1) We thereby call down God's mercy upon our country and world.

2) We also obtain the divine help which is necessary for virtue and peace in society.

**14. Why should a family pray together?**

1) To obtain the graces they need, especially the grace to keep the Catholic Faith.

2) To ask God to bless them as a family.

3) To imitate the Holy Family (Jesus, Mary and Joseph).

4) To give good example to the children.

5) To keep the family together.

*"For where there are two or three gathered together in my name, there am I in the midst of them."* (Matthew 18:20).

**15. How often should a family pray together?**

At least once a day, preferably after the evening meal, when all the members of the family are together.

*"A family that prays together stays together."* (Father Peyton).

**16. Why do Catholics have statues and pictures of Our Lord, the Blessed Virgin and the Saints?**

1) Because they wish to honor them, just as we honor public heroes.

2) Because it is easier to pray to them when looking at a picture or a statue of them.

3) Because it helps Catholics raise their minds frequently to God during the day.

## PRACTICAL POINTS

**1.** There are two main kinds of prayer, vocal and mental. Vocal prayer uses set formulas, such as the *Our Father* and the *Hail Mary.* Mental prayer is praying without words, which is also called meditation.

**2.** It is good to pray during the day with short prayers, such as, "Jesus, I love You"; "My God, I offer this hour of work for my sins"; "My Jesus, mercy."

**3.** It is not necessary to kneel while praying, but it certainly is much easier to pray when on your knees.

# *Lesson 5:* Public Worship of God

*Note: As a creature of God, you are bound to pray to Him, not only as an individual, but also as a member of society. The chief form of public worship in the Catholic Church is the Mass, which is explained in this lesson. A fuller explanation will be given in Lesson 23.*

## 1. What happens at Mass?

The priest changes bread and wine into the Body and Blood of Jesus Christ and offers them to God the Father.

## 2. Who said the first Mass?

Jesus Christ, right after the Last Supper on the night before He died, nearly 2000 years ago.

> *"And whilst they were at supper, Jesus took bread, and blessed, and broke: and gave to his disciples, and said: Take ye, and eat. This is my body. And taking the chalice, he gave thanks, and gave to them, saying: Drink ye all of this. For this is my blood."* (Matthew 26:26-28).

## 3. How could Jesus change bread and wine into His Body and Blood?

Because He is God, as will be shown in Lesson 15.

## 4. Did Jesus give this power to anyone?

Yes, to His twelve Apostles.

> *"Do this for a commemoration of me."* (Luke 22:19).

## 5. Did Jesus want His Apostles to hand down this power to others?

Yes, because He wanted all men of all times to have the holy Sacrifice and to eat His Body and drink His Blood.

> *"Except you eat the flesh of the Son of man, and drink his blood, you shall not have life in you."* (John 6:54).

**6. How did the Apostles hand down this power?**

By making other men priests and bishops. (See Lesson 28.)

**7. Who has this power today?**

The priests and bishops of the Catholic Church.

**8. At what part of the Mass does the priest change bread and wine into the Body and Blood of Jesus Christ?**

At the Consecration, about the middle of Mass, when he says "This is My Body." "This is the chalice of My Blood..."

## PRACTICAL POINTS

1. The Mass until recent years was said in Latin because Latin is the official language of the Church and was the official and universal language in many parts of the world two thousand years ago; also, because it is a language that does not change. (Mass is also said in several other sacred languages, such as Greek and Old Slavonic.) Today it is usually said in the language of the people, but in some places it is still said in the traditional Latin. In the old missals (books containing the Mass prayers) you will find the Mass prayers in both Latin and English.

2. The clothes worn by the priest at Mass, called vestments, are a special priestly type of garb that has a relationship to the vestments worn by the priests of the Old Testament. These vestments are symbolic of the unchangeableness of the Church.

3. One cannot lay down set rules about how to pray at Mass because the Mass may be followed word-for-word, as in the missal, or in spirit, according to what is going on in the various parts of the Mass, or by practicing one's private devotions.

4. The difference between High Mass and Low Mass is that at High Mass the priest sings some of the Mass prayers; whereas, at Low Mass he does not sing.

**5.** Catholics are obliged to attend Mass every Sunday and on the six Holy Days of Obligation. (See Page 137). To miss Mass on these days is a mortal sin.

**6.** Other forms of public worship are Benediction of the Blessed Sacrament, novenas and Lenten services.

# $\mathcal{L}esson$ 6: Angels and Devils

*"And I beheld, and I heard the voice of many angels round about the throne, and the living creatures, and the ancients; and the number of them was thousands of thousands, saying with a loud voice: The Lamb that was slain is worthy to receive power, and divinity, and wisdom, and strength, and honour, and glory, and benediction."* (Apocalypse 5:11-12).

**1. What is an angel?**

An angel is a spirit, that is, a creature who does not have a body.

**2. Is an angel a real person?**

Yes, because an angel has a mind and a will.

**3. How do you know there are angels?**

The Bible mentions angels about three hundred times.

**4. Why did God create the angels?**

To serve Him in Heaven, to act as His messengers to man, and to act as guardians over human beings.

**5. Does everyone have a guardian angel?**

Yes, God appoints an angel to watch over every human being.

> *"See that you despise not one of these little ones: for I say to you, that their angels in heaven always see the face of my Father who is in heaven."* (Matthew 18:10).

**6. What does your guardian angel do for you?**

Your angel prays for you, protects you from evil and inspires you to do good.

> *"Behold I will send my angel, who shall go before thee, and keep thee in thy journey, and bring thee into the place that I have prepared. Take notice of him, and hear his voice."* (Exodus 23:20-21).

## 7. Did all the Angels obey God?

No, some of them, led by Lucifer, or Satan, disobeyed God and were sent immediately into Hell. These are the fallen angels or devils.

*"And there was a great battle in heaven, Michael and his angels fought with the dragon, and the dragon fought and his angels. And they prevailed not, neither was their place found any more in heaven."* (Apocalypse 12:7-8).

## 8. Is there really a devil?

Yes, the Bible often speaks of the devil as a real person.

*"And that great dragon was cast out, that old serpent, who is called the devil and Satan, who seduceth the whole world."* (Apocalypse 12:9).

## 9. How does the devil act toward human beings?

The devil tempts people to commit sin.

*"Be sober and watch: because your adversary the devil, as a roaring lion, goeth about seeking whom he may devour. Whom resist ye, strong in faith: knowing that the same affliction befalls your brethren who are in the world."* (1 Peter 5:8-9).

## 10. How can you fight the devil?

The best weapons against the devil are prayer (especially calling on Jesus and Mary), holy water, blessed medals, scapulars and other blessed objects.

*"Put you on the armour of God, that you may be able to stand against the deceits of the devil. For our wrestling is not against flesh and blood; but against principalities and powers, against the rulers of the world of this darkness, against the spirits of wickedness in the high places."* (Ephesians 6:11-12).

## PRACTICAL POINTS

1. Your guardian angel is a real person, who is always with you to help and protect you. Pray to him often and thank him for his help. Your guardian angel is an indication of how much God loves and cares for you.

2. The devil has succeeded in getting a large number of people to think of him as a Halloween ghost. He is a real person and is a real danger to you personally.

**3.** Not all your temptations come from the devil. Others come from your own flesh ("concupiscence") and from the world about you—traditionally stated, "from the world, the flesh and the devil."

# Lesson 7:
## Human Beings and the Purpose of Life

*"Lay not up to yourselves treasures on earth: where the rust, and moth consume, and where thieves break through and steal. But lay up to yourselves treasures in heaven: where neither the rust nor moth doth consume, and where thieves do not break through, nor steal. For where thy treasure is, there is thy heart also."* (Matthew 6:19-21).

**1. What is a human being?**

A creature who has a body and a soul.

*"Thou hast made him a little less than the angels, thou hast crowned him with glory and honour."* (Psalm 8:6).

**2. What is the soul?**

It is the spiritual part of man, that part which will never die.

*"God said, 'Let us make man to our image and likeness.'"* (Genesis 1:26).

**3. Where is your soul?**

In every part of you that is alive.

**4. Is your soul real?**

Yes, just as real as your body.

**5. How do you know you have a soul?**

You can do spiritual things: you can think, do things without being forced, decide not to do things, make things, enjoy a joke or a book or a movie, talk, work out mathematical problems, etc.

*An animal cannot do any of these things. That which makes you able to do them is your soul.*

**21**

**6. Where did your soul come from?**

God created your soul and joined it to the tiny body in your mother's womb.

*"And the Lord God formed man of the slime of the earth: and breathed into his face the breath of life, and man became a living soul."* (Genesis 2:7).

**7. How long will your soul and body stay together?**

Until death, which is the separation of body and soul.

*"And the dust return into its earth, from whence it was, and the spirit return to God who gave it."* (Ecclesiastes 12:7). *"Watch ye therefore, because you know not the day nor the hour."* (Matthew 25:13).

**8. What will happen to your body when you die?**

It will rot away to the earth from which it came.

*"For dust thou art, and into dust thou shalt return."* (Genesis 3:19).

**9. What will happen to your soul when you die?**

It will be judged by God and will go to Heaven, to Purgatory or to Hell.

*"It is appointed unto men once to die, and after this the judgment."* (Hebrews 9:27).

**10. Will your soul ever be joined to your body again?**

Yes, on Judgment Day God will call your body back from the earth and join it to your soul. This will be the resurrection of the body at the end of the world.

*"Behold, I tell you a mystery. We shall all indeed rise again: but we shall not all be changed. In a moment, in the twinkling of an eye, at the last trumpet: for the trumpet shall sound, and the dead shall rise again incorruptible."* (1 Corinthians 15:51-52).

**11. After the Resurrection, will your soul and body be always together?**

Yes, both body and soul will be together forever, either in Heaven or in Hell.

*"For we must all be manifested before the judgment seat of Christ, that every one may receive the proper things of the body, according as he hath done, whether it be good or evil."* (2 Corinthians 5:10).

## 12. When will Judgment Day be?

Nobody but God knows this.

*"But of that day and hour no one knoweth, no not the angels of heaven, but the Father alone."* (Matthew 24:36).

## 13. How should you prepare for Judgment Day?

Pray constantly, obey all of God's commandments, and do penance for your sins.

*"And take heed to yourselves, lest perhaps your hearts be overcharged with surfeiting and drunkenness, and the cares of this life, and that day come upon you suddenly. For as a snare shall it come upon all that sit upon the face of the whole earth. Watch ye, therefore, praying at all times, that you may be accounted worthy to escape all these things that are to come, and to stand before the Son of man."* (Luke 21:34-36).

## 14. What, then, is the true purpose of life?

To live your life according to God's plan and thus to save your soul.

*"For what shall it profit a man, if he gain the whole world, and suffer the loss of his soul? Or what shall a man give in exchange for his soul?"* (Mark 8:36-37). *"Behold, now you that say: Today or tomorrow we will go into such a city, and there we will spend a year, and will traffic, and make our gain. Whereas you know not what shall be on the morrow. For what is your life? It is a vapour which appeareth for a little while, and afterwards shall vanish away. For that you should say: If the Lord will, and if we shall live, we will do this or that."* (James 4:13-15).

# $\mathcal{L}$εᴧᴧon 8: Sanctifying Grace

*And Jesus addressed them, and spoke to them again in parables, saying "The kingdom of heaven is likened to a king, who made a marriage for his son...And the marriage was filled with guests. And the king went in to see the guests: and he saw there a man who had not on a wedding garment. And he saith to him: Friend, how camest thou in hither not having on a wedding garment? But he was silent. Then the king said to the waiters: Bind his hands and feet and cast him into the exterior darkness: there shall be weeping and gnashing of teeth."* (Matthew 22:1-13).

### 1. Why did God make you?

God made you to know, love and serve Him in this world so that you might share in His happiness in Heaven.

### 2. Are mere human beings equipped to share God's happiness?

No, because God has a completely different kind of life.

*To share in the happiness of another, it is necessary to have the same kind of life. A dog, for example, cannot enjoy a book because man has a higher kind of life than a dog.*

### 3. How is God's life a higher kind of life than that of man?

God's life is unlimited, uncreated and independent; whereas, human life is very limited, created by God and absolutely dependent on Him.

*"For in him we live, and move, and are."* (Acts 17:28).

### 4. What, then, is needed to share in God's happiness?

A new kind of life, called Sanctifying Grace.

## 5. What is Sanctifying Grace?

A sharing in the life of God, which raises you to God's level and gives you the power to share in His happiness.

*"By whom he hath given us the most great and precious promises: that by these you may be made partakers of the divine nature."* (2 Peter 1:4).

## 6. Does Sanctifying Grace make you the same as God?

No, only like God, because Sanctifying Grace is a *created* sharing in the life of God.

*You are still a human being, but one that is equipped to live in Heaven.*

## 7. Can you get into Heaven without Sanctifying Grace?

No, it is absolutely impossible to live in Heaven without Sanctifying Grace.

*The wedding garment in the parable* (Matthew 22:10-13) *is Sanctifying Grace. The banquet hall is Heaven, and the king is God. The attendants are the Angels, and the darkness outside is Hell.*

## 8. Is there Sanctifying Grace in your soul when you are born?

No, all human beings are created without Sanctifying Grace.

*"For all have sinned, and do need the glory of God. Being justified freely by his grace, through the redemption, that is in Christ Jesus."* (Romans 3:23-24).

## 9. How can you get Sanctifying Grace?

Baptism puts Sanctifying Grace into your soul for the first time.

*"Unless a man be born again of water and the Holy Ghost, he cannot enter into the kingdom of God."* (John 3:5).

## 10. Can you make Sanctifying Grace grow in your soul?

Yes, chiefly by receiving Holy Communion and the other Sacraments, and by prayer and good works.

*"But grow in grace, and in the knowledge of our Lord and Saviour Jesus Christ."* (2 Peter 3:18).

## 11. Can you lose Sanctifying Grace?

Yes, by committing a serious sin (that is, a mortal sin)—one that destroys God's life in your soul.

*"But sin, when it is completed, begetteth death."* (James 1:15).

## 12. Can you feel Sanctifying Grace in your soul?

No, because Sanctifying Grace is completely spiritual.

*It is impossible to experience something spiritual, such as grace, a soul, an angel, with the five senses.*

## 13. Does a religious feeling indicate Sanctifying Grace in the soul?

No, nor does the absence of such a feeling indicate the absence of Sanctifying Grace.

*A person being baptized may not experience a religious feeling but can be morally certain from the promise of Christ that Baptism is putting Sanctifying Grace into his soul.*

## PRACTICAL POINTS

1. Adam and Eve were created with Sanctifying Grace in their souls. After them, the only other human being created with Sanctifying Grace was the Blessed Virgin Mary, the Mother of Jesus.

2. A soul in the state of Grace has two kinds of life: human life, and the sharing in God's life. A mortal sin kills (or drives out) only the Sanctifying Grace. Nothing can kill the *human* life of the soul, which is immortal.

3. Babies who die without being baptized cannot go to Heaven because they die without Sanctifying Grace. The Church has never taught, as an official doctrine, what happens to the souls of unbaptized infants. However, Catholic books approved by the Church have consistently taught that unbaptized babies probably go to a place of natural happiness in the next world called Limbo. God is not cruel or unjust in not allowing them to enter Heaven because Sanctifying Grace is a gift, and no one has a right to a gift. Man does not have a *natural* right to Heaven, which is a *supernatural* end for man. If a baby dies without Baptism, the parents should put the matter in God's hands and trust in His wisdom and goodness.

4. Adults who, through their own fault, neglect to be baptized, do not go to Limbo but to Hell.

# $\mathcal{L}$*esson* 9: Heaven

*"Behold what manner of charity the Father hath bestowed upon us, that we should be called, and should be the sons of God. Therefore the world knoweth not us, because it knew not him. Dearly beloved, we are now the sons of God; and it hath not yet appeared what we shall be. We know, that, when he shall appear, we shall be like to him: because we shall see him as he is."* (1 John 3:1-2).

### 1. What is Heaven?

The place of perfect happiness in the next world.

*"Eye hath not seen, nor ear heard, neither hath it entered into the heart of man, what things God hath prepared for those that love him."* (1 Corinthians 2:9).

### 2. Who will go to Heaven?

Only those who have Sanctifying Grace in their souls at the moment of death.

*"Then shall the king say to them that shall be on his right hand: Come, ye blessed of my Father, possess you the kingdom prepared for you from the foundation of the world."* (Matthew 25:34).

### 3. What is the happiness of Heaven?

It will consist in seeing God face to face and possessing Him in divine love.

*"We see now through a glass in a dark manner; but then face to face. Now I know in part; but then I shall know even as I am known."* (1 Corinthians 13:12).

### 4. Why is the happiness of Heaven perfect?

Because God made you for Himself and you can find perfect satisfaction in Him alone.

*"Thou hast made us for Thyself, O Lord, and our hearts are restless until they rest in Thee."* (St. Augustine).

**5. Will everyone have the same happiness in Heaven?**

No, the happiness of some will be greater than that of others, but everyone will be as happy as he can be.

**6. Why will some have greater happiness than others?**

Because some will see God more clearly.

*"For the Son of man shall come in the glory of his Father with his angels, and then he will render to every man according to his works."* (Matthew 16:27).

**7. Why will some see God more clearly?**

Because they died with more Sanctifying Grace in their souls.

*"And every man shall receive his own reward, according to his own labour."* (1 Corinthians 3:8).

**8. How, then, should you spend your time on earth?**

Try to get as much Sanctifying Grace in your soul as you can before you die.

*"Labour not for the meat which perisheth, but for that which endureth unto life everlasting, which the Son of man will give you."* (John 6:27). *"The night cometh, when no man can work."* (John 9:4).

**9. Will there be any sorrow or pain in Heaven?**

No, nor will there be any sickness, temptation or sin, but complete, unending joy.

*"And God shall wipe away all tears from their eyes: and death shall be no more, nor mourning, nor crying, nor sorrow shall be any more."* (Apocalypse 21:4).

**10. Will you know your family and friends in Heaven?**

Yes, and also the Angels and Saints.

*"Now therefore you are no more strangers and foreigners; but you are fellow citizens with the saints, and the domestics of God."* (Ephesians 2:19).

**11. What would keep you from getting into Heaven?**

Dying with a serious (i.e., mortal) sin on your soul.

*"And there shall not enter into it any thing defiled, or that worketh abomination or maketh a lie, but they that are written in the book of life of the Lamb."* (Apocalypse 21:27).

## 12. How often should you pray to get into Heaven?

Every day, since getting into Heaven is the purpose of life.

*"As the hart panteth after the fountains of water; so my soul panteth after thee, O God. My soul hath thirsted after the strong living God; when shall I come and appear before the face of God?"* (Psalm 41:2-3).

## 13. What is the chief difference between Heaven and Limbo?

The souls in Heaven see God face to face; whereas, those in Limbo do not.

*Seeing God face to face is called the Beatific Vision. It contains all possible happiness and is unending.*

## PRACTICAL POINTS

1. You will never get bored or used to Heaven because God is unlimited in every way. Nothing on this earth can completely satisfy you, whether it is money or fame or pleasure, since everything created is limited.

2. Thinking often of Heaven, putting it before everything else, will give you the correct scale of values, as well as peace of mind in this world.

# $\mathcal{L}$ελλon 10: Mortal and Venial Sin

*"Let no man, when he is tempted, say that he is tempted by God. For God is not a tempter of evils, and he tempteth no man. But every man is tempted by his own concupiscence, being drawn away and allured. Then when concupiscence hath conceived, it bringeth forth sin. But sin, when it is completed, begetteth death."* (James 1:13-15).

**1. What is sin?**

Sin is any thought, word, desire, action or neglect (omission) forbidden by the law of God.

**2. When are you guilty of sin?**

To be guilty—

1) you must know that you are breaking God's law, and

2) you must freely choose to do it.

**3. How many kinds of sin are there?**

Two—mortal sin and venial sin.

**4. What is mortal sin?**

A "big" sin, a serious violation of God's law.

*Examples: Getting drunk, adultery, stealing something expensive.*

**5. What does mortal sin do to the soul?**

It drives the Sanctifying Grace out of your soul.

*"What fruit had you then in those things, of which you are now ashamed? For the end of them is death."* (Romans 6:21).

**6. Where will you go if you die with mortal sin on your soul?**

You will go to Hell forever.

*"They shall have their portion in the pool burning with fire and brimstone, which is the second death."* (Apocalypse 21:8).

**7. Can all mortal sins be forgiven?**

Yes, if you are truly sorry for them and do everything necessary for forgiveness.

*"If we confess our sins, he is faithful and just, to forgive us our sins, and to cleanse us from all iniquity."* (1 John 1:9).

**8. What is venial sin?**

A "small" sin, a less serious violation of God's law.

*Examples: Impatience, ordinary anger, stealing something cheap, getting slightly drunk.*

**9. What does venial sin do to your soul?**

It does not drive out the Grace from your soul, but it does make you less pleasing to God.

**10. Where will you go if you die with venial sin on your soul?**

You will go to Purgatory.

**11. Can a number of venial sins become a mortal sin?**

No. (Except that a *series* of similar small, recurring thefts from the same person amounts to one large theft and therefore can be a mortal sin.)

**12. If you do something wrong, but do not know it is wrong, are you guilty of sin?**

No, if it is through no fault of yours that you do not know it is wrong.

*Example: If you eat meat on Ash Wednesday, completely forgetting that it is Ash Wednesday, you are not guilty of sin.*

**13. Are you guilty of sin if you intend to do something wrong, even though you do not actually do it?**

Yes, because even the intention to offend God is a sin.

*Example: You intend to rob a bank but are frightened off by the guards.*

### 14. What should you do if you do not know whether something is mortal or venial sin?

You should not do it; otherwise, you will commit a mortal sin, because you show yourself willing to offend God seriously.

*Example: You do not know whether eating too much is a mortal or venial sin, but you go ahead and eat too much anyway.*

### 15. What is temptation?

Temptation is an attraction to commit sin.

### 16. Can you always overcome temptation?

Yes, because no temptation can force you into sin, and God will always help you.

*"And God is faithful, who will not suffer you to be tempted above that which you are able: but will make also with temptation issue, that you may be able to bear it."* (1 Corinthians 10:13).

### 17. What should you do when you are tempted?

First, ask God to help you, and then, get busy doing something else.

*"And lead us not into temptation. But deliver us from evil."* (Matthew 6:13).

### 18. How can you avoid temptations?

Avoid all persons, places or things that may lead you into sin, and ask God for actual graces.

### 19. What are actual graces?

They are "helps" from God which enlighten the mind and strengthen the will to do good and avoid evil.

*"My grace is sufficient for thee: for power is made perfect in infirmity."* (2 Corinthians 12:9).

Actual graces come and go, but Sanctifying Grace remains in the soul. Sanctifying Grace is LIFE, actual grace is HELP.

### 20. Can you resist actual graces?

Unfortunately, yes, for you are free, and God does not force you to use them.

*"And we helping do exhort you, that you receive not the grace of God in vain."* (2 Corinthians 6:1).

# _Lesson 11:_  Hell

_"The Son of Man shall send his angels, and they shall gather out of his kingdom all scandals, and them that work iniquity. And shall cast them into the furnace of fire: there shall be weeping and gnashing of teeth."_ (Matthew 13:41-42).

### 1. What is Hell?

The place in the next world where the souls of the damned are condemned to suffer forever with the devils.

> _"If any one abide not in me, he shall be cast forth as a branch, and shall wither, and they shall gather him up, and cast him into the fire, and he burneth."_ (John 15:6).

### 2. How do you know that there is a Hell?

The Bible and Tradition often speak of the everlasting punishments of Hell.

> _"Then he shall say to them also that shall be on his left hand: Depart from me, you cursed, into everlasting fire which was prepared for the devil and his angels. And these shall go into everlasting punishments: but the just, into life everlasting."_ (Matthew 25:41-46).

### 3. Who will go to Hell?

Only those who die with mortal sin on their souls, that is, without Sanctifying Grace.

> _"And whosoever was not found written in the book of life, was cast into the pool of fire."_ (Apocalypse 20:15).

### 4. Does anyone ever get out of Hell?

No, Hell is a place of "everlasting punishment." (Matthew 25:46).

> _"And the smoke of their torments shall ascend up for ever and ever: neither have they rest day nor night."_ (Apocalypse 14:11).

**33**

### 5. What are the pains of Hell?

Separation from God, torture by fire, regret, and the companionship of the devils.

*"Before I go, and return no more, to a land that is dark and covered with the mist of death: a land of misery and darkness, where the shadow of death, and no order, but everlasting horror dwelleth."* (Job 10:21-22).

### 6. What is the pain of separation from God?

To be separated from God, the Source of all love and happiness, will be the greatest pain in Hell.

*"The Lord Jesus shall be revealed from heaven, with the angels of his power: in a flame of fire, giving vengeance to them who know not God, and who obey not the gospel of our Lord Jesus Christ. Who shall suffer eternal punishment in destruction, from the face of the Lord, and from the glory of his power."* (2 Thessalonians 1:7-9).

### 7. Is there real fire in Hell?

Yes, Jesus often spoke of the "unquenchable fire" of Hell and says that the damned souls will be "salted with fire" (Mark 9:43), which is "everlasting fire" (Matthew 25:41).

*"If any one abide not in me, he shall be cast forth as a branch, and shall wither, and they shall gather him up, and cast him into the fire, and he burneth."* (John 15:6).

### 8. How does the fire in Hell differ from the fire here on earth?

The fire in Hell burns without consuming and can torture not only the body but the soul as well.

*"Where their worm dieth not, and the fire is not extinguished."* (Mark 9:47). *"Humble thy spirit very much: for the vengeance on the flesh of the ungodly is fire and worms."* (Ecclesiasticus 7:19).

### 9. What is the pain of regret?

The pain of regret means that you will be tortured forever with the thought that you had so many chances to save your soul and be happy with God, but lost Heaven because of mortal sin.

**10. What is the pain of the companionship of the devils?**

Your companions in Hell will be the devils and the other lost souls, who will always hate you and mock you for being such a fool.

*"Then he shall say to them also that shall be on his left hand: Depart from me, you cursed, into everlasting fire which was prepared for the devil and his angels."* (Matthew 25:41).

**11. Are the pains of Hell the same for all?**

All the souls in Hell will have the same type of punishment, but the degree of suffering will differ according to the number and kind of sins committed.

## PRACTICAL POINTS

**1.** Think often of Hell and the possibility of your going there. Pray every day that you will not die with mortal sin on your soul. Say the *Act of Contrition* every night (Page 159).

**2.** Presumption is the sin committed by people who think that a good God will not punish a sinner with the torments of Hell. God, being a just judge, has to reject those who choose to separate themselves from Him by mortal sin.

**3.** The horror of Hell helps us understand the evil of mortal sin. Mortal sin is the greatest evil in the universe.

# $\mathcal{L}$εᴋᴋon 12:   Purgatory

"And the day following Judas [Machabeus] came with his company, to take away the bodies of them that were slain, and to bury them with their kinsmen, in the sepulchres of their fathers. And they found under the coats of the slain some of the donaries of the idols of Jamnia, which the law forbiddeth to the Jews: so that all plainly saw, that for this cause they were slain. Then they all blessed the just judgment of the Lord, who had discovered the things that were hidden. And so betaking themselves to prayers, they besought him, that the sin which had been committed might be forgotten. But the most valiant Judas exhorted the people to keep themselves from sin, forasmuch as they saw before their eyes what had happened, because of the sins of those that were slain. And making a gathering, he sent twelve thousand drachms of silver to Jerusalem for sacrifice to be offered for the sins of the dead, thinking well and religiously concerning the resurrection, (for if he had not hoped that they that were slain should rise again, it would have seemed superfluous and vain to pray for the dead), and because he considered that they who had fallen asleep with godliness, had great grace laid up for them. It is therefore a holy and wholesome thought to pray for the dead, that they may be loosed from sins." (2 Machabees 12:39-46).

### 1. What is Purgatory?

A place and state of temporary punishment in the next world.

> Hell, on the other hand, is a place of eternal or everlasting punishment.

### 2. What does the word "Purgatory" mean?

It means "cleansing" (or "purging"): Purgatory is a place where the soul is cleansed of unforgiven venial sin and/or the "debt" of sins already forgiven but not yet made up for ("atoned" for).

**3. How do you know that there is a Purgatory?**

The constant teaching and practice of the Catholic Church, based on the Bible and Tradition, and even common sense, prove the existence of Purgatory.

**4. How does common sense indicate the existence of Purgatory?**

Only people with mortal sin go to Hell, and on the other hand, no one can enter Heaven with even the smallest sin. Therefore, there must be a place in the next world where lesser sins can be taken off the soul.

**5. Who will go to Purgatory?**

People who die with Sanctifying Grace in their souls, but—

1) who die with venial sin on their souls, or

2) who have not completed (satisfied for) the punishment still due to their already-forgiven sins.

**6. What is meant by the "punishment still due to sin"?**

This means that, even though God forgives your sins, He still requires that you be punished for them (i.e., "pay" for them), either in this life or in the next.

*For example, a boy playing ball in his yard breaks his neighbor's window. He goes and tells the lady he is sorry, and she forgives him—but, she tells him he will still have to pay for the window.*

**7. Do you suffer in Purgatory?**

Yes, besides not being allowed to see God face to face, the souls in Purgatory suffer a great deal.

*"The fire of Purgatory," says St. Augustine, "is more terrible than man can suffer in this life."*

**8. How long will you have to suffer in Purgatory?**

That depends on the number and seriousness of the sins to be atoned for.

*"Amen I say to thee, thou shalt not come out from thence till thou repay the last farthing." (Matthew 5:26).*

### 9. Where do you go when you leave Purgatory?

To Heaven to see God and enjoy Him forever.

*"My soul hath thirsted after the strong living God; when shall I come and appear before the face of God?"* (Psalm 41:3).

### 10. Will Purgatory ever end?

Yes, at the Last Judgment. After that you will go to Heaven forever.

### 11. Can you help the souls in Purgatory?

You can shorten their stay by having Masses said for them, by praying for them and by doing good works for them.

*"Have pity on me, have pity on me, at least you my friends, because the hand of the Lord hath touched me."* (Job 19:21).

### 12. Does the Bible say anything about praying for the dead?

Yes, we read that Judas Machabeus "sent twelve thousand drachms of silver to Jerusalem for sacrifice to be offered for the sins of the dead." (2 Machabees 12:43).

### 13. How can you avoid Purgatory?

Avoid even the smallest faults, do penance for sins already forgiven, gain indulgences and receive Extreme Unction. (See Chapter 26.)

## PRACTICAL POINTS

1. All Souls' Day is the day set aside by the Church for special prayers and Masses for all the souls suffering in Purgatory. It is celebrated every year on November 2.

2. The souls in Purgatory cannot help themselves. We should help them by our prayers and sacrifices. They, in turn, can and do pray for us.

3. The souls in Purgatory are known as the Poor Souls.

# $\mathcal{L}$εϩϩοn 13: Original Sin

*"Wherefore as by one man sin entered into this world, and by sin death; and so death passed upon all men, in whom all have sinned...For as by the disobedience of one man, many were made sinners; so also by the obedience of one, many shall be made just."* (Romans 5:12,19).

Read the first three chapters of *Genesis.*

**1. What is Original Sin?**

The sin committed by Adam, the father of the human race. By Original Sin, Adam lost Sanctifying Grace.

**2. Who were Adam and Eve?**

The first man and woman, from whom every human being on this earth is descended.

**3. How did the sin of Adam affect the human race?**

Because of Adam's sin, every human being is created with Original Sin on his soul and without Sanctifying Grace, since Adam was the father of the human race.

Adam's nature became "fallen" through Original Sin, and we his descendants inherit his fallen nature. *"By the disobedience of one man, many were made sinners."* (Romans 5:19).

**4. What else did Adam's sin do?**

The gates of Heaven were closed; disease, pain and death came into the world; the mind of man was darkened and his will was weakened.

*"For the imagination and thought of man's heart are prone to evil from his youth."* (Genesis 8:21).

**5. Is Heaven still closed to the human race?**

No, because of Christ's death on the Cross, God reopened Heaven and made Sanctifying Grace available to man.

*"As in Adam all die, so also in Christ all shall be made alive."* (1 Corinthians 15:22).

### 6. What happened to the good people who died before Christ?

They went to Limbo, a place of natural happiness in the next world, and stayed there until Jesus ascended into Heaven.

*"And it came to pass, that the beggar died, and was carried by the angels into Abraham's bosom. And the rich man also died: and he was buried in hell."* (Luke 16:22).

### 7. How do you get rid of Original Sin and obtain Sanctifying Grace?

Baptism takes away Original Sin and puts Sanctifying Grace into your soul.

*"Unless a man be born again of water and the Holy Ghost, he cannot enter into the kingdom of God."* (John 3:5).

### 8. Was any human being preserved from Original Sin?

Yes, the Blessed Virgin Mary, whose soul was created with Sanctifying Grace in it. This is called the Immaculate Conception.

*"And the angel being come in, said unto her: Hail, full of grace, the Lord is with thee: blessed art thou among women."* (Luke 1:28).

### PRACTICAL POINTS

1. From the way God punished the sin of Adam, it is clear that the sin was a serious one. If Adam had not committed it, there would have been no disease, pain or death. So, you can see what a terrible thing sin is in the eyes of God.

2. Only unbaptized babies and unbaptized persons who never had the use of their minds go to Limbo now.

3. Baptism does not restore the other gifts lost by Adam's sin, that is, freedom from pain, disease and death, and the perfect control over the lower nature.

4. The Church teaches that the human race began with one man and one woman. Any scientific theory of man's biological origin must square with this fact.

# $\mathcal{L}$ε $\mathcal{ss}$οη $14$: Jesus Christ, Our Saviour

*"For God so loved the world, as to give his only begotten Son; that whosoever believeth in him, may not perish, but may have life everlasting. For God sent not his Son into the world, to judge the world, but that the world may be saved by him."* (John 3:16-17).

## 1. Did God abandon the human race after Adam's sin?

No, He promised to send a saviour into the world and to open again the gates of Heaven.

> *"I will put enmities between thee and the woman, and thy seed and her seed: she shall crush thy head, and thou shalt lie in wait for her heel."* (Genesis 3:15).

## 2. Who is the Saviour of all men?

Jesus Christ, who, by His death on the Cross, has saved us from our sins.

> *"Thou shalt call his name Jesus. For he shall save his people from their sins."* (Matthew 1:21).

## 3. Who is Jesus Christ?

The Son of God, the Second Person of the Holy Trinity, true God and true man.

> *"And I saw, and I gave testimony, that this is the Son of God."* (John 1:34).

## 4. Who is the Mother of Jesus?

The Blessed Virgin Mary.

> *"And the angel said to her: Fear not, Mary, for thou hast found grace with God. Behold thou shalt conceive in thy womb, and shalt bring forth a son; and thou shalt call his name Jesus."* (Luke 1:30-31).

**5. Did Jesus have a human father?**

No, because Mary conceived Jesus through the power of God.

*"Therefore the Lord himself shall give you a sign. Behold a virgin shall conceive, and bear a son, and his name shall be called Emmanuel."* (Isaias 7:14).

**6. Who, then, was St. Joseph?**

He was only the foster father of Jesus.

*"The angel of the Lord appeared to him in his sleep, saying: 'Joseph, son of David, fear not to take unto thee Mary thy wife, for that which is conceived in her, is of the Holy Ghost.'"* (Matthew 1:20).

**7. Did Mary have any other children besides Jesus?**

No, she and Joseph lived as brother and sister, although they were legally married.

*"The angel Gabriel was sent from God...to a virgin espoused to a man whose name was Joseph...and the virgin's name was Mary...and the angel said unto her...'Thou shalt conceive in thy womb, and shalt bring forth a son'...And Mary said to the angel: 'How shall this be done, because I know not man?'"* (Luke 1:26-34).

**8. When and where was Jesus born?**

He was born some 2,000 years ago on Christmas Day in Bethlehem, a small town near Jerusalem in Israel.

**9. Where did Jesus live during most of His life?**

In the city of Nazareth, until He was about thirty years old.

**10. How did Jesus spend the last three years of His life?**

He preached His Gospel, worked miracles and established His Church.

*"And Jesus went about all Galilee, teaching in their synagogues, and preaching the gospel of the kingdom: and healing all manner of sickness and every infirmity, among the people."* (Matthew 4:23).

## 11. How was Jesus condemned to death?

One of His Apostles, Judas Iscariot, betrayed Jesus to His enemies, who got the Roman governor, Pontius Pilate, to condemn Him to death, as He had foretold.

*"Jesus began to shew to his disciples, that he must go to Jerusalem, and suffer many things from the ancients and scribes and chief priests, and be put to death, and the third day rise again."* (Matthew 16:21).

## 12. What were the chief sufferings of Jesus?

The agony in the garden, the bloody sweat, the cruel scourging, the crowning with thorns, His death on the Cross, and His spiritual and mental sufferings.

*"He was wounded for our iniquities, he was bruised for our sins: the chastisement of our peace was upon him, and by his bruises we are healed."* (Isaias 53:5).

## 13. How did Jesus die?

He was nailed to a cross on a hill called Calvary, just outside the city of Jerusalem, and three hours later He died.

*"Who his own self bore our sins in his body upon the tree: that we, being dead to sins, should live to justice: by whose stripes you were healed."* (1 Peter 2:24).

## 14. On what day did Jesus die?

On Good Friday.

*"This is my commandment, that you love one another, as I have loved you. Greater love than this no one hath, that a man lay down his life for his friends."* (John 15:12-13).

## 15. When Jesus died, where did His soul go?

He went to Limbo to tell the people there that the gates of Heaven would soon be opened.

*"Put to death indeed in the flesh, but enlivened in the spirit. In which also coming he preached to those spirits that were in prison."* (1 Peter 3:18-19).

**43**

### 16. On what day did Jesus rise from the dead?

On Easter Sunday, three days after His death, as He had foretold.

*"For I delivered unto you first of all, which I also received: how that Christ died for our sins, according to the scriptures: And that he was buried, and that he rose again the third day, according to the scriptures: And that he was seen by Cephas; and after that by the eleven. Then was he seen by more than five hundred brethren at once."* (1 Corinthians 15:3-6).

### 17. How long did Jesus stay on earth after His Resurrection?

For forty days, to prove that He really had risen.

*"To whom also he shewed himself alive after his passion, by many proofs, for forty days appearing to them, and speaking of the kingdom of God."* (Acts 1:3).

### 18. When did Jesus ascend into Heaven?

On Ascension Thursday, forty days after His Resurrection.

*"And the Lord Jesus, after he had spoken to them, was taken up into heaven, and sitteth on the right hand of God."* (Mark 16:19).

### 19. Who ascended into Heaven with Jesus?

The souls who had been in Limbo.

*"Ascending on high, he led captivity captive; he gave gifts to men. Now that he ascended, what is it, but because he also descended first into the lower parts of the earth?"* (Ephesians 4:8-9).

### 20. Will Jesus come back again?

Yes, on Judgment Day, to judge the living and the dead.

*"For the Son of Man shall come in the glory of his Father with his angels: and then will he render to every man according to his works."* (Matthew 16:27).

### 21. What did the Apostles do after the Ascension?

They went back to Jerusalem and waited for the coming of the Holy Ghost.

*"But when the Paraclete cometh, whom I will send you from the Father, the Spirit of truth, who proceedeth from the Father, he shall give testimony of me."* (John 15:26).

## 22. When did the Holy Ghost come down upon the Apostles?

On Pentecost Sunday, ten days after the Ascension.

*"And when the days of the Pentecost were accomplished, they were all together in one place: And suddenly there came a sound from heaven, as of a mighty wind coming, and it filled the whole house where they were sitting. And there appeared to them parted tongues as it were of fire, and it sat upon every one of them: And they were all filled with the Holy Ghost."* (Acts 2:1-4).

## PRACTICAL POINTS

1. The life of Jesus is contained in the first four books of the New Testament, called the Gospels, written by Matthew, Mark, Luke and John. However, only the main events of Christ's life are in the Gospels.

2. The brothers and sisters of Jesus mentioned in the Bible were not children of Mary, but were only cousins. The words "brother" and "sister" were used by the Jews to mean cousin or other relative. See *Leviticus* 10:4, *1 Paralipomenon (1 Chronicles)* 23:22, *Genesis* 12:5 and *Genesis* 14:14.

3. From the sufferings of Jesus, you should learn of God's great love for man, the evil of sin and the perfect example of patience in suffering. "For what glory is it, if committing sin, and being buffeted for it, you endure? But if doing well you suffer patiently; this is thankworthy before God. For unto this are you called: because Christ also suffered for us, leaving you an example that you should follow his steps." (*1 Peter* 2:20-21). "And he said to all, 'If any man will come after me, let him deny himself, and take up his cross daily, and follow me.'" (*Luke* 9:23).

# Lesson 15:

## Jesus Christ, True God and True Man

*"Again the high priest asked him, and said to him: Art thou the Christ the Son of the blessed God? And Jesus said to him: I am. And you shall see the Son of man sitting on the right hand of the power of God, and coming with the clouds of heaven. Then the high priest rending his garments, saith: What need we any further witnesses? You have heard the blasphemy. What think you? Who all condemned him to be guilty of death."* (Mark 14:61-64).

### 1. Who is Jesus Christ?

Jesus Christ is the Son of God, the Second Person of the Holy Trinity, true God and true Man.

*"But when the fulness of the time was come, God sent his Son, made of a woman, made under the law: that he might redeem them who were under the law: that we might receive the adoption of sons."* (Galatians 4:4-5).

### 2. Is Jesus Christ really God?

Yes. He is equal to God the Father and equal to God the Holy Ghost.

*"And lo, the heavens were opened to him: and he saw the Spirit of God descending as a dove, and coming upon him. And behold a voice from heaven, saying: This is my beloved Son, in whom I am well pleased."* (Matthew 3:16-17). *"Going therefore, teach ye all nations; baptizing them in the name of the Father, and of the Son, and of the Holy Ghost."* (Matthew 28:19).

### 3. Did Jesus say that He was God?

Yes, He said this to His Apostles and the people and also while under oath in the Sanhedrin court.

*"I and the Father are one."* (John 10:30). *"Jesus saith to them: But whom do you say that I am? Simon Peter answered and said: Thou art Christ, the Son of the living God."* (Matthew 16:15-16).

## 4. How did Jesus prove that He is God?

Chiefly by His miracles.

*"If I do not the works of my Father, believe me not. But if I do, though you will not believe me, believe the works: that you may know and believe that the Father is in me, and I in the Father."* (John 10:37-38).

## 5. What is a miracle?

In general, a miracle is an unusual event which is contrary to or beyond the laws of nature and which cannot be explained except through the power of God.

*"The works themselves, which I do, give testimony of me, that the Father hath sent me."* (John 5:36).

## 6. Could science in years to come explain away miracles?

Never, because only through the power of God could blindness be cured instantly or the dead come back to life just by the sound of a voice.

*"From the beginning of the world it hath not been heard, that any man hath opened the eyes of one born blind. Unless this man were of God, he could not do any thing."* (John 9:32-33).

## 7. How do miracles prove a statement to be true?

A miracle can be performed only by the power of God, and God could not perform a miracle in favor of a lie.

*"For the works which the Father hath given me to perfect; the works themselves, which I do, give testimony of me, that the Father hath sent me. And the Father himself who hath sent me, hath given testimony of me."* (John 5:36-37).

## 8. What were some of the miracles of Jesus?

He cured six blind men, eleven lepers, two paralytics, a deaf mute, raised three people from the dead, cast the devil out of many, changed water into wine, calmed a storm, walked on the waters of the sea, twice fed thousands of people with a few loaves of bread and a few fish—a word, a look, a gesture, a simple touch, and all nature obeyed Him as its Master.

*"Many other signs also did Jesus in the sight of his disciples, which are not written in this book. But these are written, that you may believe that Jesus is the Christ, the Son of God: and that believing, you may have life in his name."* (John 20:30-31).

**47**

**9. What was the greatest miracle of Jesus?**

His resurrection from the dead, as He had foretold.

*"To whom also he shewed himself alive after his passion, by many proofs, for forty days appearing to them, and speaking of the kingdom of God." (Acts 1:3).*

**10. In what other ways did Jesus prove that He was God?**

By the holiness of His life, by the perfection of His teaching, by His prophecies and by fulfilling the prophecies of the Old Testament.

**11. What is a prophecy?**

A sure foretelling of a future event which cannot be naturally foreseen, except through the power of God.

**12. Were the prophecies of the Old Testament fulfilled in Jesus?**

Yes, some of them were about His origin, nationality, tribe, divinity, time and place of birth, the virginity of His Mother, His flight into Egypt, His betrayal, and practically all the details of His Passion and death, agony, scourging, mockery, Crucifixion, burial and Resurrection.

**13. What are some of the prophecies made by Jesus?**

The following have already been fulfilled: those about His Passion, death, Resurrection, denial by Peter, betrayal of Judas, the coming of the Holy Ghost, the persecution of His followers, the destruction of the Temple and Jerusalem and the preaching of the Gospel throughout the whole world.

**14. What value do these prophecies have?**

Like the miracles, they prove that Jesus was telling the truth when He said He was God.

*"The works that I do in the name of my Father, these give testimony of me." (John 10:25).*

**15. Is Jesus a real man?**

Yes, because He has a body and a soul.

**16. Is Jesus a human person?**

No, He is a divine Person, the Second Person of the Holy Trinity.

*Jesus Christ has two natures, a human nature and a divine nature, and yet He is only one Person.*

**17. Is Jesus Christ both God and man?**

Yes, He is God from all eternity, but He became man some two thousand years ago.

*"For in him dwelleth all the fulness of the Godhead corporeally."* (Colossians 2:9).

**18. Why did God become man?**

To save man from his sins and to open again the gates of Heaven.

*"Jesus Christ came into the world to save sinners."* (1 Timothy 1:15).

**19. How did Jesus save man?**

By His death on the Cross.

*"Knowing that you were not redeemed with corruptible things as gold or silver, from your vain conversation of the tradition of your fathers: but with the precious blood of Christ."* (1 Peter 1:18-19).

**20. Are you automatically saved by the death of Jesus?**

No, because His death merely makes it possible for you to be saved.

*"With fear and trembling work out your salvation."* (Philippians 2:12).

**21. What is necessary to be saved?**

You have to be baptized, belong to the Church established by Jesus Christ, obey the Ten Commandments, receive the Sacraments, pray, do good works and die with Sanctifying Grace in your soul.

*"Not every one that saith to me, Lord, Lord, shall enter into the kingdom of heaven: but he that doth the will of my Father who is in heaven, he shall enter into the kingdom of heaven."* (Matthew 7:21).

# $\mathcal{L}$esson 16:

## The Catholic Church Is
## The Only True Church

*"Whom do you say that I am? Simon Peter answered and said: Thou art Christ, the Son of the living God. And Jesus answering, said to him: Blessed art thou, Simon Bar-Jona: because flesh and blood hath not revealed it to thee, but my Father who is in heaven. And I say to thee: That thou art Peter; and upon this rock I will build my church, and the gates of hell shall not prevail against it."* (Matthew 16:16-18).

### JESUS GIVES HIS AUTHORITY TO THE APOSTLES

*"And Jesus coming, spoke to them, saying: All power is given to me in heaven and in earth. Going therefore, teach ye all nations; baptizing them in the name of the Father, and of the Son, and of the Holy Ghost. Teaching them to observe all things whatsoever I have commanded you: and behold I am with you all days, even to the consummation of the world."* (Matthew 28:18-20).

**1. Can you learn to save your soul just by reading the Bible?**

No, because certain things in the Bible can be misunderstood and because the Bible does not include everything God taught.

*"Understanding this first, that no prophecy of scripture is made by private interpretation."* (2 Peter 1:20). *"As also in all his [St. Paul's] epistles, speaking in them of these things; in which are certain things hard to be understood, which the unlearned and unstable wrest [twist], as they do also the other scriptures, to their own destruction."* (2 Peter 3:16).

**2. What did Jesus do to make sure that His teaching would never be misunderstood?**

He established a church.

*"The house of God, which is the church of the living God, the pillar and ground of the truth."* (1 Timothy 3:15).

**3. When did Jesus establish His Church?**

Nearly two thousand years ago.

**4. How many churches did Jesus establish?**

Only one.

*"Upon this rock I will build my church."* (Matthew 16:18). *"There shall be one fold and one shepherd."* (John 10:16).

**5. How long did Jesus plan His Church to last?**

Until the End of the World.

*"I am with you all days, even to the consummation of the world."* (Matthew 28:20).

**6. How did Jesus establish His Church?**

By giving His authority to the Apostles to rule and to teach.

*"Teaching them to observe all things whatsoever I have commanded you."* (Matthew 28:20).

**7. Did the people have to obey the Apostles?**

Yes, because they spoke with the authority of Jesus, and therefore, to disobey them would be a sin.

*"He that heareth you, heareth me; and he that despiseth you, despiseth me; and he that despiseth me, despiseth him that sent me."* (Luke 10:16).

**8. Did the authority of the Apostles die with them?**

No, they handed down their authority to others, since Jesus instituted His Church to last until the End of the World.

*Some of the men who received authority from the Apostles: Matthias (Acts 1:22), Paul and Barnabas (Acts 13:2), Timothy, Silas, Sylvanus, Titus, Luke, Mark (Acts 17:14; 2 Corinthians 1:19; 2 Timothy 14:11).*

**9. Which church today has this same authority?**

The Catholic Church, because it is the only Church established by Jesus Christ.

**10. How do you know the Catholic Church is the only true church?**

History shows that it is the only church that can be traced back to Christ.

**11. Does everyone have to obey the Catholic Church?**

Yes, because she alone has the authority of Jesus to rule and to teach.

*To disobey the Catholic Church knowingly is just as much a sin as to disobey Jesus Christ or His Apostles.*

**12. Where did the Protestant churches come from?**

They were established by men who had no authority to start churches of their own.

**13. Who started the first Protestant church?**

The first Protestant church was established less than 500 years ago in Germany by Martin Luther, in 1520.

**14. Name the founders of other leading Protestant churches.**

| Name of Church | Founder | When Founded | Where Founded |
|---|---|---|---|
| Episcopalian | King Henry VIII | 1534 | England |
| Presbyterian | John Knox | 1560 | Scotland |
| Congregationalist | Robert Browne | 1583 | England |
| Baptist | John Smith | 1600 | Holland |
| Methodist | John Wesley | 1739 | England |
| Adventist | William Miller | 1831 | New York |
| Christian Scientist | Mary Baker Eddy | 1879 | Massachusetts |

## PRACTICAL POINTS

1. A non-Catholic who suspects that the Catholic Church is the one true Church of God and does not investigate her claims with a mind to join if her claims prove to be true cannot be saved, because outside of Christ's Mystical Body (which is the Catholic Church) there is no salvation.

2. A "non-Catholic" who, through no fault of his own, does not realize that the Catholic Church is the only true Church and who dies with Sanctifying Grace in his soul, will go to Heaven, since "Christ died for all" (*2 Corinthians* 5:15) and "will have all men to be saved, and to come to the knowledge of the truth." (*1 Timothy* 2:4). Still, those who are not visibly members of the Catholic Church have many difficulties trying to save their souls without the guidance of that Church which cannot teach error and without her Sacraments, of which Baptism imparts the life of God to the soul (Sanctifying Grace) and the other Sacraments add to the Sanctifying Grace in the soul, take away sins, and also give other graces that enable a person to do good and avoid sin.

3. You should try to bring others "to the knowledge of the truth" (*1 Timothy* 2:4) by prudently suggesting that they take instructions in the True Religion.

# $\mathcal{L}$essoη 17:

## Qualities of the Catholic Church

*"And he gave some apostles, and some prophets, and other some evangelists, and other some pastors and doctors, for the perfecting of the saints, for the work of the ministry, for the edifying of the body of Christ: Until we all meet into the unity of faith, and of the knowledge of the Son of God, unto a perfect man, unto the measure of the age of the fulness of Christ; that henceforth we be no more children tossed to and fro, and carried about with every wind of doctrine by the wickedness of men, by cunning craftiness, by which they lie in wait to deceive. But doing the truth in charity, we may in all things grow up in him who is the head, even Christ."* (Ephesians 4:11-15).

**1. What kind of church did Jesus intend to establish?**

A church that would be universal, united and holy, one that could not teach error and that could not be destroyed.

**2. Which is the only church that has these qualities?**

Only the Catholic Church.

**3. What does the word "Catholic" mean?**

It means "universal," embracing all.

**4. Why is the Church of Jesus called "Catholic"?**

Because it is 1) for all people, 2) of all nations, 3) of all times and because 4) it teaches all the doctrines of Jesus.

*"Going therefore, teach ye all nations; baptizing them in the name of the Father, and of the Son, and of the Holy Ghost. Teaching them to observe all things whatsoever I have commanded you."* (Matthew 28:19-20).

## 5. When was the name "Catholic" first used of the Church of Jesus?

In the year 110, by St. Ignatius, bishop of Antioch, who wrote: "Where Jesus Christ is, there is the Catholic Church." (*Ad Smyrn.* 8:2).

*"The Church is called Catholic by all her enemies, as well as by her own children. Heretics and schismatics can call the Church by no other name than Catholic, for they would not be understood, unless they used the name by which the Church is known to the whole world."* (St. Augustine, 4th-5th Centuries, in *De Vera Religione*—"Concerning True Religion").

## 6. Is the Catholic Church spread all over the world?

Yes, its approximately 1,000,000,000 members are from all races and all colors and all sections of the world.

*The marvelous growth of the Church, in spite of great obstacles and fierce persecution, is certainly a sign that it is the Church of Jesus Christ.*

## 7. What is meant by the unity of the Catholic Church?

This unity means that all Catholics worldwide—

1) believe the same things,

2) obey the same laws,

3) receive the same Sacraments,

4) worship at the same Holy Sacrifice of the Mass,

5) are all united under the same authority, that of the Pope in Rome.

*"And not for them only do I pray, but for them also who through their word shall believe in me; that they all may be one, as thou, Father, in me, and I in thee; that they also may be one in us."* (John 17:20-21).

## 8. Why is the Catholic Church holy?

It is holy because—

1) its Founder, Jesus Christ, is holy,

2) it teaches a holy doctrine,

3) it gives its members what is needed to lead a holy life,

4) thousands of its members, from every walk of life, from every race and from every period of history, have become Saints.

**9. Why cannot the Catholic Church ever teach error?**

Because Jesus Christ promised to be always with His Church to protect it from error.

*"Going therefore, teach ye all nations...Teaching them to observe all things whatsoever I have commanded you: and behold I am with you all days, even to the consummation of the world."* (Matthew 28:19-20).

**10. Has the Catholic Church ever changed its teaching?**

No, for some 2,000 years the Catholic Church has taught the same things which Jesus Christ taught.

*"The Church of the living God, the pillar and ground of the truth."* (1 Timothy 3:15).

**11. Why can the Catholic Church never be destroyed?**

Because Jesus promised that "the gates of hell shall not prevail against it." (Matthew 16:18).

*"The God of heaven will set up a kingdom that shall never be destroyed."* (Daniel 2:44).

**12. Has anyone ever tried to destroy the Church?**

Yes, as Jesus Christ foretold, many governments have tried without success to destroy the Church, and thousands of Catholics (martyrs) have died for the True Church.

*"They will deliver you up in councils, and they will scourge you in their synagogues. And you shall be brought before governors, and before kings for my sake...and you will be hated by all men for my name's sake."* (Matthew 10:17-22).

### FALSE SLOGANS

1. "All religions are good." *Answer:* There is only one religion, as far as God is concerned, since He established only one, not three hundred. All other religions were established by men who had no authority from God to start them. A religion is either true or false, just as a dollar bill is either genuine or counterfeit. Although a religion may have some truth, it is a false religion if it was established by a man.

2. "It doesn't make any difference what church you belong to." *Answer:* It certainly does make a difference whether you belong to the one established by God or to one established by a man. It makes a difference whether you belong to the church that has everything necessary to lead you to Heaven, or not.

3. "All religions teach the same thing and believe in the same God." *Answer:* All religions disagree on the important teachings of Jesus Christ. Some teach that He is God; others say He is not. Some teach that you have to be baptized to get into Heaven; others deny the necessity of Baptism. Some teach that Baptism really takes away sin, while others hold that it is only a symbol. If all religions believed in the same God, they would all have to teach the same things, since God cannot contradict Himself. God is not the author of confusion and contradiction, but of clear, unchangeable Truth. "Jesus Christ, yesterday and today, and the same for ever. Be not led away with various and strange doctrines." (*Hebrews* 13:8-9).

4. "It doesn't matter what you believe; it's how you act that counts." *Answer:* It does matter, because you act according to your belief. It does matter whether you believe killing a person dying of an incurable disease is a sin or not, or whether marriage is to last until death or not. God has given the human race certain, definite truths to believe, and He expects everyone to believe them. "He that believeth and is baptized, shall be saved: but he that believeth not shall be condemned." (*Mark* 16:16). He told His Apostles: "Going therefore, teach ye all nations...teaching them to observe *all* things whatsoever I have commanded you." (*Matthew* 28:19-20).

## PRACTICAL POINTS

1. If you are convinced that the Catholic Church is the only true Church, then you have an obligation to join it; otherwise, you cannot be saved. However, joining the Church is a very serious step, because in so doing,

you place yourself completely and forever under the authority of the Church in all things concerning religion. This means that you promise to believe everything the Church teaches, to worship the way the Catholic Church worships, and to obey all the laws of the Church.

2. It is not unreasonable to place yourself under the authority of the Catholic Church, because its authority is from God. "He who heareth you, heareth me; and he who despiseth you, despiseth me; and he who despiseth me, despiseth him who sent me." (*Luke* 10:16).

3. By joining the Catholic Church, you can be sure of what you have to believe and do in order to save your soul, and you will be able to lead a good life and attain salvation with the graces flowing from the Sacraments and the countless other sources of spiritual strength provided by God's Church. Besides, you will have the peace of mind that comes only from knowing that you are doing God's will. "For you were as sheep going astray; but you are now converted to the shepherd and bishop of your souls." (*1 Peter* 2:25).

# *Lesson 18:* The Pope, Vicar of Christ

*"Jesus saith to them: But whom do you say that I am? Simon Peter answered and said: Thou art Christ, the Son of the living God. And Jesus answering, said to him: Blessed art thou, Simon Bar-Jona: because flesh and blood hath not revealed it to thee, but my Father who is in heaven. And I say to thee: That thou art Peter; and upon this rock I will build my church, and the gates of hell shall not prevail against it. And I will give to thee the keys of the kingdom of heaven. And whatsoever thou shalt bind upon earth, it shall be bound also in heaven; and whatsoever thou shalt loose on earth, it shall be loosed also in heaven."* (Matthew 16:15-19).

**1. What did Jesus do to make sure His Church would always be united?**

He put one man in complete charge of His Church.

*"If a kingdom be divided against itself, that kingdom cannot stand. And if a house be divided against itself, that house cannot stand."* (Mark 3:24-25).

**2. Who has complete charge of the Church?**

The Pope, who is the bishop of Rome and the Vicar (agent) of Christ on earth.

**3. Who is the Pope?**

The Pope is the visible head of the whole Catholic Church.

*"And I will set up one shepherd over them, and he shall feed them."* (Ezechiel 34:23).

**4. Who was the first Pope?**

St. Peter, who was made Pope by Jesus Christ Himself.

**59**

**5. When did Jesus promise to make Peter the Pope?**

Several months before He died.

*"Thou art Peter, and upon this rock I will build my Church."* (Matthew 16:18).

**6. When did Jesus actually make Peter the first Pope?**

Shortly before He ascended into Heaven, Jesus gave Peter complete authority over the whole Church.

*"Jesus said to Simon Peter, 'Feed my lambs...feed my lambs...feed my sheep.'"* (John 21:15-17).

**7. Did Peter's authority die with him?**

No, it was handed down to a man named Linus, and after he died (78 A.D.), it was handed down to Cletus (d. 90 A.D.), and then to Clement (d. 100 A.D.), and after that to another, and so on, during the past nearly 2,000 years.

*"Where Peter is, there is the Church."* (St. Ambrose, in the 4th Century).

**8. Do all Catholics have to obey the Pope?**

Yes, because he speaks with the authority of Christ.

*Catholics, however, have to obey the Pope only in regard to matters of religion.*

**9. Can the Pope make an error when teaching religion?**

No, not when he speaks as head of the whole Church.

*"Simon, Simon...I have prayed for thee, that thy faith fail not: and thou, being once converted, confirm thy brethren."* (Luke 22:31-32).

## GOVERNMENT OF THE CHURCH

The Pope, also called our Holy Father and the Sovereign Pontiff, lives in Vatican City, which is in Rome, Italy. St. Peter died in Rome, and ever since then, the Bishop of Rome has been the Pope. When the Pope dies, the Cardinals elect his successor. There have been 264 Popes so far.

The world is divided up into territories called dioceses. Each diocese is ruled over by a bishop. A diocese is divided into parishes, which are ruled over by pastors. A pastor may have one or several priests to assist him.

## PRACTICAL POINTS

1. Papal infallibility means that the Pope, when speaking as head of the whole church on matters of faith or morals, cannot teach error. Infallibility is not to be confused with impeccability, which means that one cannot commit sin. The Pope is not impeccable; he can sin.

2. One of the reasons why there are so many different kinds of Protestants (over 300 kinds) is that there is no Protestant church that has one man holding complete authority from God. They are "like sheep that have no shepherd." (*Matthew* 9:36). We should pray for them. "Other sheep I have, that are not of this fold: them also I must bring, and they shall hear my voice, and there shall be one fold and one shepherd." (*John* 10:16).

# THE 7 SACRAMENTS

It is important that you know whether you have Sanctifying Grace in your soul or not. It is something you cannot afford to be uncertain about. Grace, however, is absolutely spiritual. You cannot feel it or experience it with any of the five senses. A religious feeling does not indicate the presence of Sanctifying Grace in the soul. Therefore, Jesus Christ had to give us some signs which would indicate that Grace is going into the soul. He had to give us signs that we could see, feel, hear or experience with some of the five senses. As a matter of fact, He gave us seven such signs by which we could know that we are receiving Grace. These signs are the seven Sacraments.

The Sacraments are another indication of how much God loves you and how interested He is in you. In the following lessons, you will realize keenly how much non-Catholics have missed in life, as the wonders of God's loving care are unfolded before your eyes.

# $\mathcal{L}$ε♪♪οπ 19: The Seven Sacraments

## GETTING INTO HEAVEN IS THE ONLY THING THAT MATTERS

*"Therefore I say to you, be not solicitous for your life, what you shall eat, nor for your body, what you shall put on. Is not the life more than the meat: and the body more than the raiment? Behold the birds of the air, for they neither sow, nor do they reap, nor gather into barns: and your heavenly Father feedeth them. Are not you of much more value than they? And which of you by taking thought, can add to his stature one cubit? And for raiment why are you solicitous? Consider the lilies of the field, how they grow: they labour not, neither do they spin. But I say to you, that not even Solomon in all his glory was arrayed as one of these. And if the grass of the field, which is today, and tomorrow is cast into the oven, God doth so clothe: how much more you, O ye of little faith?*

*"Be not solicitous therefore, saying, What shall we eat: or what shall we drink, or wherewith shall we be clothed? For after all these things do the heathens seek. For your Father knoweth that you have need of all these things. Seek ye therefore first the kingdom of God, and his justice, and all these things shall be added unto you."* (Matthew 6:25-33).

### 1. What is absolutely necessary to get to Heaven?

You have to have Sanctifying Grace in your soul when you die. Sanctifying Grace is God's life in the soul.

### 2. How do you obtain Sanctifying Grace?

One of the chief ways of obtaining Sanctifying Grace is by receiving the Sacraments.

### 3. What is a Sacrament?

An outward sign made by Jesus Christ to give you grace.

*"I am come that they may have life, and may have it more abundantly."* (John 10:10).

### 4. What is an "outward sign"?

Anything which you can see (or hear or feel), which tells you about something you cannot see.

*For example, a barber pole is an outward sign which you can see in front of a store. It tells you that there is a barber inside whom you cannot see.*

### 5. How are the Sacraments outward signs?

The outward sign of the Sacrament of Baptism, for example, is the pouring of the water on your head and saying the words, "I baptize thee in the name of the Father and of the Son and of the Holy Ghost."

*You can see the priest pour the water, and you can hear him say those words. This is the outward sign that you are receiving Sanctifying Grace, which you cannot see or hear or feel.*

### 6. How are the Sacraments different from other outward signs?

The Sacraments not only *tell* you that you have Grace in your soul, but they actually *put* the Grace into it.

*All other signs only tell you about something you cannot see. A barber pole cannot give you a haircut; it only tells you that there is a barber inside the shop.*

### 7. Name the Seven Sacraments.

Baptism, Confirmation, Holy Eucharist, Penance, Extreme Unction, Holy Orders, and Matrimony.

### 8. Describe the Seven Sacraments.

BAPTISM takes away Original Sin and gives you Sanctifying Grace for the first time.

CONFIRMATION gives you the Holy Ghost and makes you a strong Catholic.

HOLY EUCHARIST is the Body and Blood of Jesus Christ.

PENANCE (or Confession) takes away sins committed after Baptism.

EXTREME UNCTION prepares you for death.

HOLY ORDERS gives a man the powers of the priesthood.

MATRIMONY unites a couple in Christian marriage and gives them the graces they need to obey God's laws on marriage.

**9. Do the Sacraments always give grace?**

Yes, if you receive them worthily.

**10. Give some examples of receiving Sacraments unworthily.**

Receiving Holy Communion, Marriage, Holy Orders with a mortal sin on your soul. Not telling all your mortal sins in Confession.

**11. What kind of sin is it to receive a Sacrament unworthily?**

A mortal sin and a sacrilege.

**12. Where do the Sacraments get the power to give grace?**

From God, because only God can make an outward sign (like the pouring of water) able to put grace into the soul.

*"I am the way, and the truth, and the life."* (John 14:6).

**13. What else do the Sacraments give besides Sanctifying Grace?**

Special help called "sacramental grace."

*For example, Confirmation gives you the strength to be a loyal Catholic; Matrimony gives you the special help to live your married life according to God's laws.*

**14. How many times can you receive Baptism, Confirmation and Holy Orders?**

You can receive these Sacraments only once.

*Moreover, only qualified Catholic men can receive Holy Orders.*

**15. Why can you receive these Sacraments only once?**

Because they imprint on the soul a spiritual mark called a character.

*This mark stays on the soul after death for the glory of those who are saved and for the shame of those who are lost.*

**16. How many times may you receive Holy Communion and Penance?**

Every day, if you want.

*Many Catholics receive these Sacraments once a week.*

**17. How often can you receive the Sacrament of Matrimony?**

Only once, unless your marriage partner dies.

**18. How often can you receive Extreme Unction?**

Any time you are in danger of death from sickness, old age or accident.

**19. Who gives you the Sacraments?**

The priest gives you Baptism, Holy Communion, Penance (Confession) and Extreme Unction.

*Ordinarily, the bishop gives Confirmation, but in a real emergency your pastor can give it. Only a bishop can give Holy Orders. The bride and groom give the Sacrament of Matrimony to each other, although a priest and two witnesses have to be present. In an emergency, anyone, even a non-Catholic, can baptize.*

## PRACTICAL POINTS

1. Except in the case of babies being baptized (they receive the smallest amount of grace), the better you prepare yourself to receive a Sacrament, the greater the amount of grace you will obtain.

2. Christ gave His Church only the essential parts of each Sacrament, but the Church has surrounded each Sacrament with beautiful ceremonies, which together with the administration of the Sacraments themselves and the Mass ceremonies, form what is called the *Liturgy* of the Church.

3. The Sacraments give grace automatically, as long as the priest or bishop and the one receiving the Sacraments fulfill all the required conditions. It is really Jesus Christ who gives the Sacrament.

4. The Bible speaks about the Sacraments, grace, the Mass, etc., but it uses different words for these things. (For example, in one place Our Lord calls Sanctifying Grace "living water.")

# *Lesson 20:*

## The Sacrament of Baptism

*"And there was a man of the Pharisees, named Nicodemus, a ruler of the Jews. This man came to Jesus by night, and said to him: Rabbi, we know that thou art come a teacher from God; for no man can do these signs which thou dost, unless God be with him. Jesus answered, and said to him: Amen, amen I say to thee, unless a man be born again, he cannot see the kingdom of God. Nicodemus saith to him: How can a man be born when he is old? Can he enter a second time into his mother's womb, and be born again? Jesus answered: Amen, amen I say to thee, unless a man be born again of water and the Holy Ghost, he cannot enter into the kingdom of God."* (John 3:1-5).

### 1. What is Baptism?

Baptism is the Sacrament which makes you a Christian and a member of the Catholic Church and gives you the right to receive the other Sacraments.

### 2. What does Baptism do to your soul?

1) It takes away all sin: Original Sin, plus mortal and venial sins.

> *"Do penance and be baptized every one of you in the name of Jesus Christ for the remission of your sins."* (Acts 2:38).

2) It puts Sanctifying Grace into your soul for the first time.

3) It brings the Holy Ghost to dwell in your soul.

4) It makes you a member of the Catholic Church.

5) It enables you to receive the other Sacraments.

### 3. Why do you have to be baptized?

Because Jesus Christ said, "Unless a man be born again of water and the Holy Ghost, he cannot enter into the kingdom of God." (*John* 3:5).

### 4. What kind of sin is it to delay your Baptism?

A serious (mortal) sin if you are convinced that the Catholic Church is the only true Church.

*"Why tarriest thou? Rise up, and be baptized, and wash away thy sins."* (Acts 22:16).

### 5. What do you have to do to be baptized?

1) You have to take a full course of instructions in the Catholic religion;

2) give up all seriously sinful habits;

3) have the right intention.

*The "right intention" means that you wish to become a Catholic because the Catholic Church is the only true Church.*

### 6. Who gives Baptism?

Ordinarily, the priest, but anyone can baptize in an emergency. (See Lesson 33, Q. 4, p. 126).

### 7. How is Baptism given?

It is given by pouring water over the forehead of the person to be baptized and saying while pouring the water, "I baptize thee in the name of the Father and of the Son and of the Holy Ghost" (*Matthew* 28:19), while having at least the mininum intention to do what the Church wants you to do by performing this sacramental act.

*Baptism can also be given by immersion or sprinkling, but in all cases the water has to flow over the head or forehead (not just the hair).*

### 8. What are sponsors for?

Sponsors at Baptism are supposed to see that their god-children stay faithful to their religious duties.

*A sponsor has to be a good Catholic at least fourteen years old.*

### 9. Why do you take the name of a Saint at Baptism?

You take a Saint's name to have that Saint watch over you and to have someone to imitate.

*See Page 174 for a list of Saints' names.*

### 10. Do babies have to be baptized?

Yes, because they have Original Sin on their souls, which means they have no Sanctifying Grace.

### 11. How soon should a baby be baptized?

Within two or three weeks of its birth.

*It is a mortal sin to delay the Baptism of a baby for a long time.*

## PRACTICAL POINTS

1. Make arrangements with your parish priest a week before the baby's Baptism. The baby's godfather and godmother should be good Catholics.

2. An expectant mother in a hospital should tell the doctors and nurses that she is a Catholic and that, if there is any danger to the life of the baby, they should send for a priest right away. In case of real emergency, somebody should baptize the baby, even in the womb, if necessary.

3. If there is a miscarriage, the whole substance from the womb should be put into water right away, and the words, "I baptize thee in the name of the Father and of the Son and of the Holy Ghost," should be said by the one baptizing. It should be noted that the water has to flow over the skin of the fetus or embryo. Consequently, it will be necessary to break the protective membrane which encloses the body.

4. Regarding babies who die without Baptism, see Page 26, point 3.

5. If you were baptized in a Protestant church, you will probably still have to go through the Catholic ceremony of Baptism. This is called *conditional* Baptism. The reason for this is to make sure that you are

really baptized. It is practically impossible to find out if your Protestant Baptism was done according to the intention of Christ, since many Protestant ministers consider Baptism merely a sort of initiation ritual or symbol that produces no effect in the soul.

6. In exceptional cases, when Baptism of water is not possible, Baptism of blood or of desire may take its place. Baptism of blood consists in suffering death for Christ. Baptism of desire consists in an act of perfect contrition or sorrow for one's sins out of love of God (see Page 90, Q. 17), which somehow includes a desire for Baptism of water.

# $\mathcal{L}\!\text{e}\!\delta\!\delta\!\text{o}n$ 21:
## The Sacrament of Confirmation

*"Now when the apostles, who were in Jerusalem, had heard that Samaria had received the word of God, they sent unto them Peter and John. Who, when they were come, prayed for them, that they might receive the Holy Ghost. For he was not as yet come upon any of them; but they were only baptized in the name of the Lord Jesus. Then they laid their hands upon them, and they received the Holy Ghost."* (Acts 8:14-17).

### 1. What is Confirmation?
Confirmation is the Sacrament which gives you the strength to be a good Catholic.

*This Sacrament completes and perfects the Christian life you begin at Baptism.*

### 2. Who comes into your soul when you are confirmed?
The Holy Ghost, the Third Person of the Holy Trinity.

*"Or know you not, that your members are the temple of the Holy Ghost?"* (1 Corinthians 6:19).

### 3. What does Confirmation do for your soul?
1) Confirmation gives you more Sanctifying Grace;

2) it gives you more strength to stay away from sin and lead a Christian life;

3) it helps you to be a loyal and faithful follower of Jesus Christ.

4) it gives you the strength to profess your Catholic Faith openly and not to hide it.

### 4. Can you get into Heaven without Confirmation?
Yes, but it is more difficult.

**5. Is it a sin to neglect Confirmation?**

Yes, it is a sin to neglect Confirmation.

**6. Who gives Confirmation?**

Usually a bishop.

**7. What do you have to do to receive Confirmation worthily?**

1) You have to be a baptized Catholic, and

2) have no mortal sin on your soul.

*You should also be well instructed in the Catholic religion.*

**8. Do you have to have a sponsor for Confirmation?**

Yes, but not the same one you had for Baptism.

**9. How many times can you be confirmed?**

Only once.

**10. What is expected of a confirmed Catholic?**

A confirmed Catholic, by his prayers and words and good example, should try to lead others to the True Church.

**11. How is Confirmation given?**

In the traditional rite, the Bishop, holding his hands over those to be confirmed, prays for them and then makes the Sign of the Cross on the forehead of each one with the holy oil of Chrism. He then taps each person lightly on the cheek.

**12. What words does the Bishop say while confirming?**

He says: "I sign thee with the Sign of the Cross, and I confirm thee with the Chrism of salvation, in the name of the Father and of the Son and of the Holy Spirit."

**13. What is Holy Chrism?**

A mixture of olive oil and balm, consecrated by the Bishop on Holy Thursday; it is a symbol of the strength received in Confirmation.

**14. Why does the Bishop tap each one on the cheek?**

The tap on the cheek is to remind those confirmed that they must be ready to suffer all things, even death, for the sake of Jesus Christ.

*"Blessed are ye when they shall revile you, and persecute you, and speak all that is evil against you, untruly, for my sake."* (Matthew 5:11).

## PRACTICAL POINTS

1. Choose a good Catholic for your sponsor. You also have to select the name of another Saint for Confirmation (not the one you had for Baptism).

2. The Holy Ghost comes into your soul more fully when you are confirmed. He brings to your soul His Seven Gifts, which are: Wisdom, Understanding, Knowledge, Counsel, Fortitude, Piety and Fear of the Lord.

3. A dying parishioner may receive Confirmation from his pastor if the Bishop cannot be reached in time.

# $\mathcal{L}$esson 22:

## The Sacrament of the Holy Eucharist
## (Holy Communion)

### JESUS PROMISES TO GIVE THIS SACRAMENT

*"I am the bread of life. Your fathers did eat manna in the desert, and are dead. This is the bread which cometh down from heaven; that if any man eat of it, he may not die. I am the living bread which came down from heaven. If any man eat of this bread, he shall live for ever: and the bread that I will give, is my flesh, for the life of the world.*

*"The Jews therefore strove among themselves, saying: How can this man give us his flesh to eat?*

*"Then Jesus said to them: Amen, amen I say unto you: Except you eat the flesh of the Son of man, and drink his blood, you shall not have life in you. He that eateth my flesh, and drinketh my blood, hath everlasting life: and I will raise him up in the last day.*

*"For my flesh is meat indeed: and my blood is drink indeed. He that eateth my flesh, and drinketh my blood, abideth in me, and I in him. As the living Father hath sent me, and I live by the Father; so he that eateth me, the same also shall live by me. This is the bread that came down from heaven. Not as your fathers did eat manna, and are dead. He that eateth this bread, shall live for ever. These things he said, teaching in the synagogue, in Capharnaum."* (John 6:48-60).

### JESUS INSTITUTES THE EUCHARIST

*"And whilst they were at supper, Jesus took bread, and blessed, and broke: and gave to his disciples, and said: Take ye, and eat. This is my body. And taking the chalice, he gave*

**77**

*thanks, and gave to them, saying: Drink ye all of this. For this is my blood of the new testament, which shall be shed for many unto remission of sins."* (Matthew 26:26-28).

### 1. What is the Holy Eucharist?

The Holy Eucharist is the Sacrament in which Jesus Christ is really and physically present under the appearances of bread and wine.

*"The chalice of benediction, which we bless, is it not the communion of the blood of Christ? And the bread, which we break, is it not the partaking of the body of the Lord?"* (1 Corinthians 10:16).

### 2. Why is it also called "the Blessed Sacrament"?

Because it is the most blessed of all the Sacraments, since it is Jesus Christ Himself.

### 3. When did Jesus make this Sacrament?

At the Last Supper, on the night before He died.

### 4. How could Jesus change bread and wine into His Body and Blood?

Jesus Christ is God and therefore can do anything.

### 5. Did the bread and wine change their appearance?

No, the appearances of the bread and wine (taste, smell, color, size, shape, weight) did not change, even though the bread and wine were actually changed into the Body and Blood of Jesus.

*The entire substance of the bread and wine are changed into the substance of the Body and Blood of Jesus; thus the bread and wine no longer exist. This change is called Transubstantiation.*

### 6. Are both the Body and Blood of Christ present under the appearances of bread alone?

Yes, it is the living Christ who is present; that is, His Body, Blood, Soul and Divinity are present both under the appearance of bread and under the appearance of wine.

**7. Did Jesus give anyone the power of changing bread and wine into His Body and Blood?**

Yes, to His twelve Apostles at the Last Supper, when He told them, "Do this for a commemoration of me." (Luke 22:19).

**8. Did Jesus ordain that His Apostles hand this power down to others?**

Yes, because He wanted all men to eat His Flesh and drink His Blood.

"Amen, amen, I say to you: Except you eat the flesh of the Son of man, and drink his blood, you shall not have life in you." (John 6:54). (Here, "Life" means Sanctifying Grace.)

**9. How did the Apostles hand down this power?**

They handed it down by making other men priests and bishops through the Sacrament of Holy Orders. (See Lesson 28, Pages 102-106).

**10. When does the priest change bread and wine into the Body and Blood of Jesus Christ?**

At Mass, when he says, "This is My Body," and "This is the chalice of My Blood..."

**11. Where is the Blessed Sacrament kept?**

In a little safe (called a tabernacle) on the altar.

"And my tabernacle shall be with them, and I will be their God, and they shall be my people." (Ezechiel 37:27).

**12. What is Holy Communion?**

Receiving the Body and Blood, soul and divinity of Jesus Christ in the Holy Eucharist.

**13. What is necessary to receive Holy Communion worthily?**

1) You have to be a baptized Catholic;

2) have no mortal sin on your soul;

3) be fasting.

**14. Do you have to go to Confession first every time you receive Communion?**

No, unless you have mortal sin on your soul.

**15. What kind of sin is it to receive Communion unworthily?**

To do so knowingly and willingly is a mortal sin called a sacrilege.

> *"Therefore whosoever shall eat this bread, or drink the chalice of the Lord unworthily, shall be guilty of the body and of the blood of the Lord. But let a man prove himself: and so let him eat of that bread, and drink of the chalice. For he that eateth and drinketh unworthily, eateth and drinketh judgment to himself, not discerning the body of the Lord."* (1 Corinthians 11:27-29).

**16. What does "fasting" mean?**

"Fasting" means that, for one hour before receiving Communion, you have to stop eating solid food and drinking all liquids except water.

> *You may take water, and if sick, medicine any time before receiving. You must stop chewing gum at least one hour before. Until the 1950's, the Church required fasting from midnight before Communion; this rule was later shortened to three hours for food and one hour for liquids (with water being allowed at any time); then it was changed to one hour for food and drink, except water. It is very praiseworthy to continue observing the traditional fast either from midnight or for three hours.*

**17. How often do you have to receive Communion?**

At least once a year, during the Easter Season, that is, any time from the 6th Sunday before Easter to the 8th Sunday after Easter. This is called your Easter Duty.

> *The 6th Sunday before Easter is the First Sunday of Lent; the 8th Sunday after Easter is Trinity Sunday.*

**18. What kind of sin is it to miss your Easter Duty?**

A mortal sin.

**19. How often does a good Catholic receive Communion?**

A good Catholic receives Communion every Sunday, or every day, if possible, but only once on the same day.

**20. What does Holy Communion do for your soul?**

It makes the Sanctifying Grace in your soul grow.

*"Except you eat the flesh of the Son of man, and drink his blood, you shall not have life in you."* (John 6:54).

**21. What else does Communion do for you?**

1) Communion unites you with Jesus.

*"He that eateth my flesh, and drinketh my blood, abideth in me and I in him."* (John 6:57).

2) It is food for your soul, to help you love God and obey His laws.

*"Give us this day our daily bread."* (Luke 11:3).

3) It is a promise of your resurrection and future glory in Heaven.

*"He that eateth my flesh and drinketh my blood hath everlasting life: and I will raise him up in the last day."* (John 6:55).

4) It weakens your sinful inclinations.

## PRACTICAL POINTS

1. Ordinarily, you receive Communion during Mass. However, the priest may bring you Communion when you are sick at home or in the hospital.

2. Communion is called Viaticum when received when a person is in danger of death.

3. After receiving Communion, you should spend some time praying to Our Lord, adoring Him, thanking Him, loving Him, and asking His help. Some prayers are on Pages 158-167.

4. You are not forbidden to receive Communion with venial sins on your soul, but you are advised to recite the *Confiteor* or *Act of Contrition* before receiving. (See Pages 159-160).

**5.** In receiving Communion under the form of bread only, you receive the Blood of Jesus, as well as His Body, since His Body and Blood cannot be separated. (Catholics of the Eastern rites traditionally receive Communion under the form of bread and wine.)

**6.** Some devotions to Jesus in the Blessed Sacrament are: Benediction, Holy Hours, Forty Hours' Devotion, visits to Our Lord in the church.

# _Lesson 23:_ The Sacrifice of the Mass

## FORETOLD BY MALACHIAS THE PROPHET

*"For from the rising of the sun even to the going down, my name is great among the Gentiles, and in every place there is sacrifice, and there is offered to my name a clean oblation: for my name is great among the Gentiles, saith the Lord of hosts."* (Malachias 1:11).

## THE SACRIFICE OF THE CROSS

*"And it was almost the sixth hour; and there was darkness over all the earth until the ninth hour. And the sun was darkened, and the veil of the temple was rent in the midst. And Jesus crying with a loud voice, said: Father, into thy hands I commend my spirit. And saying this, he gave up the ghost."* (Luke 23:44-46).

## THE SACRIFICE OF THE MASS

*"For I have received of the Lord that which also I delivered unto you, that the Lord Jesus, the same night in which he was betrayed, took bread, and giving thanks, broke, and said: Take ye, and eat: this is my body, which shall be delivered for you: this do for the commemoration of me. In like manner also the chalice, after he had supped, saying: This chalice is the new testament in my blood: this do ye, as often as you shall drink, for the commemoration of me. For as often as you shall eat this bread, and drink the chalice, you shall shew the death of the Lord, until he come."* (1 Corinthians 11:23-26).

### 1. What is the Mass?

The unbloody re-enactment of the sacrifice which Christ offered to God on Calvary—but which He now offers through the priest under the appearances of bread and wine.

## 2. What is a sacrifice?

A sacrifice is the offering of a gift to God by a priest, and the destruction of the gift.

## 3. Can there be true religion without sacrifice?

No, because true religion has to have some external, public act by which men can demonstrate their worship of God.

## 4. Were there sacrifices before the coming of Jesus Christ?

Yes, God made Aaron and his sons priests and commanded them to offer sacrifices to Him.

*"But thou and thy sons look ye to the priesthood: and all things that pertain to the service of the altar, and that are within the veil, shall be executed by the priests."* (Numbers 18:7).

## 5. How were the sacrifices of the Old Testament offered?

Usually the priest would take an animal, offer it to God, kill it and then burn it on an altar.

## 6. Why were the sacrifices of the Old Testament imperfect?

They were imperfect because "it is impossible that with the blood of oxen and goats sin should be taken away." (Hebrews 10:4).

## 7. What was the perfect sacrifice?

Jesus Christ offered the perfect sacrifice when He died on the Cross.

*"But this man offering one sacrifice for sins, for ever sitteth on the right hand of God."* (Hebrews 10:12).

## 8. How was the death of Jesus Christ the perfect sacrifice?

It was perfect because both the priest and victim were not only man but also God.

*"But now once at the end of ages, he hath appeared for the destruction of sin, by the sacrifice of himself."* (Hebrews 9:26).

## 9. Did Jesus intend that His sacrifice be continued?

Yes, because He instituted the Mass, which is the re-presentation of His sacrifice on the Cross.

## 10. Who offered the first Mass?

Jesus offered the first Mass at the Last Supper when He changed bread and wine into His Body and Blood.

*"And taking bread, he gave thanks, and brake; and gave to them, saying: This is my body, which is given for you. Do this for a commemoration of me. In like manner the chalice also, after he had supped, saying: This is the chalice, the new testament in my blood, which shall be shed for you."* (Luke 22:19-20).

## 11. How is the Mass a sacrifice?

It is a sacrifice because it contains all the elements of a true sacrifice: priest and victim are Jesus Christ, and the destruction consists in the separate consecration of bread and wine into the Body and Blood of Jesus Christ.

Catholic theology teaches that "a Sacrament effects (does) what it signifies (symbolizes)." Jesus Christ died on the Cross from loss of blood; His blood is the price of our Redemption, according to Scripture and Tradition. In the Mass, the separate Consecration—first of the bread into His Body, then of the wine into His Blood—signifies the separation of Christ's body and blood, which was the cause of His death on the Cross. This signified or symbolized separation of His body and blood, therefore *effects* in the Mass the re-enactment of His death—though in the Mass, it is in an unbloody manner.

## 12. Is the sacrifice of the Mass the same as the sacrifice of the Cross?

Yes, they are the same in that the victim and the priest are the same, Jesus Christ.

*"For as often as you shall eat this bread and drink the chalice, you shall shew the death of the Lord, until he come."* (1 Corinthians 11:26).

## 13. What is the difference between the two sacrifices?

The difference is that the Sacrifice of the Cross was a bloody sacrifice; whereas, the Sacrifice of the Mass is an unbloody one.

## 14. Did Jesus Christ give anyone the power to offer Mass?

Yes, He gave it to His twelve Apostles when He said, "Do this for a commemoration of me." (Luke 22:19).

### 15. Did the Apostles say Mass?

Yes, they and their successors said Mass.

*"We have an altar, whereof they have no power to eat who serve the [Jewish] tabernacle."* (Hebrews 13:10). *"And they were persevering in the doctrine of the apostles, and in the communication of the breaking of bread, and in prayers."* (Acts 2:42).

### 16. Are there men today who can offer the Sacrifice of the Mass?

Yes, the power of offering Mass has been handed down during the past two thousand years through the Bishops of the Catholic Church, by the Sacrament of Holy Orders.

### 17. Who is the principal priest in every Mass?

Jesus Christ is the principal priest; whereas, the human priest stands in the place of Jesus and speaks His words.

*The priest we see at the altar shares in the priesthood of Jesus Christ through the Sacrament of Holy Orders.*

### 18. At what part of the Mass does the sacrifice itself take place?

At the *Consecration,* when the priest says, "This is My Body." "This is the chalice of My Blood..."

### 19. How can you offer God the perfect sacrifice?

By uniting yourself with the priest at the altar, such as by reading the Mass prayers in a missal or prayerbook.

## PRACTICAL POINTS

1. Catholics have to attend Mass every Sunday and on the six Holy Days of Obligation, which are listed on Page 137. To miss Mass deliberately on Sunday or a Holy Day is a mortal sin.

2. The Church urges her members to attend Mass every day, especially during Advent and Lent.

3. The priest may offer Mass for the souls in Purgatory. It is a custom among Catholics to have Masses said for their dead relatives and friends, instead of buying flowers. A "spiritual bouquet" of Masses not only helps the soul of the dead person but gives greater consolation to that person's relatives than flowers do.

4. The priest may also say Mass for the intentions of the living, for example, for a couple on their wedding anniversary, for the intentions of someone on his birthday, to pray for the sick, to ask for other favors, to thank God for favors received.

5. An offering of money, called a stipend, is made to the priest who says the Mass. This is not payment for the Mass but is for the support of the priest.

> *"Know you not, that they who work in the holy place, eat the things that are of the holy place; and they that serve the altar, partake with the altar? So also the Lord ordained that they who preach the gospel, should live by the gospel."* (1 Corinthians 9:13-14).

# $\mathcal{L}esson$ 24:
## The Sacrament of Penance
## (Confession)

*"Now when it was late that same day, the first of the week, and the doors were shut, where the disciples were gathered together, for fear of the Jews, Jesus came and stood in the midst, and said to them: Peace be to you. And when he had said this, he shewed them his hands and his side. The disciples therefore were glad, when they saw the Lord. He said therefore to them again: Peace be to you. As the Father hath sent me, I also send you. When he had said this, he breathed on them; and he said to them: Receive ye the Holy Ghost. Whose sins you shall forgive, they are forgiven them; and whose sins you shall retain, they are retained."* (John 20:19-23).

**1. Why did God the Father send His Son into the world?**

To save man from his sins.

*"Thou shalt call his name Jesus. For he shall save his people from their sins."* (Matthew 1:21).

**2. Does Jesus Christ have the power to forgive sins?**

Yes, Jesus has the power to forgive sin because He is God.

**3. Did Jesus Christ forgive sins while on earth?**

Yes, He forgave the sins of the paralyzed man (*Luke* 5:18-26), the woman taken in adultery (*John* 8:1-11), the sinful woman (*Luke* 7:39-50) and the good thief (*Luke* 23:39-43).

**4. Did Jesus Christ give anyone the power to forgive sin?**

Yes, to His Apostles on Easter Sunday night.

*"Whose sins you shall forgive, they are forgiven them; and whose sins you shall retain, they are retained."* (John 20:23).

**5. Did Jesus want His Apostles to hand down this power to others?**

Yes, because He died to save *all* men from their sins.

*"This is good and acceptable in the sight of God our Saviour, who will have all men to be saved."* (1 Timothy 2:3-4).

**6. How did the Apostles hand down this power to others?**

By making other men bishops and priests.

*After the Apostles died, the bishops have continued to hand down the power of forgiving sin, during the past two thousand years, through the Sacrament of Holy Orders. See the lesson on Holy Orders, Pages 102-106.*

**7. Who has the power to forgive sin today?**

All bishops and priests of the Catholic Church can forgive sin.

**8. What is the Sacrament of Penance?**

Penance is the Sacrament by which the sins committed after Baptism are forgiven.

**9. What do you have to do to have your sins forgiven?**

You have to be truly sorry for them and confess them to a Catholic priest.

*"He that hideth his sins, shall not prosper: but he that shall confess, and forsake them, shall obtain mercy."* (Proverbs 28:13).

**10. Why do you have to confess your sins to a priest?**

This is the way Jesus Christ wants sin to be forgiven.

*Otherwise, Christ would not have given His priests the power to forgive sin.*

**11. Why does the priest have to know what sins you have committed?**

He has to know whether he is to forgive your sins or "retain" them. If you are truly sorry, he will grant you forgiveness (called "absolution"); if not, he must retain them (that is, refuse to give you absolution).

89

**12. Does the priest only pray that your sins will be forgiven?**

No, the priest, by the power given him, actually takes the sins off your soul (called "absolution").

*"For what I have pardoned...I have done it in the person of Christ."* (2 Corinthians 2:10).

**13. Can you be sure that your sins are forgiven in Confession?**

Yes, if you have properly confessed them and are sorry for them.

*"If we confess our sins, he is faithful and just, to forgive us our sins, and to cleanse us from all iniquity."* (1 John 1:9).

**14. What does Confession do for your soul?**

Besides taking sin off your soul, Confession also—

1) puts Sanctifying Grace back into your soul, if you were in mortal sin;

2) makes the Grace grow, if you had only venial sins;

3) gives you extra strength to stay away from sin in the future.

**15. Can all sins be forgiven in Confession?**

Yes, if you are truly sorry for them.

**16. What is meant by "being sorry for your sins"?**

"Being sorry" means—

1) that you wish you had not committed the sins;

2) that you sincerely promise not to commit those sins again;

3) that you promise to stay away from any person, place or thing that easily leads you into sin.

**17. What kind of sorrow do you have to have to be forgiven?**

Religious sorrow, that is, you must be sorry because you dread the loss of Heaven and the pains of Hell (imperfect sorrow), and/or because you have offended the infinitely good God (perfect sorrow).

*Therefore, to have your sins forgiven, it is not enough to be sorry because your sins have caused you to lose your job or some money. The sorrow has to be religious. Sorrow for sin is called contrition. You do not have to feel the sorrow with your emotions.*

**18. Why do you not have to be afraid of Confession?**

You do not have to be afraid because—

1) you may go to any priest you want;

2) in the confessional, a screen hides you from the priest;

3) the priest is never allowed to tell anyone any sin he has ever heard in Confession. This secrecy is called the "Seal of Confession."

**19. What sins do you have to confess?**

All your mortal sins.

**20. What kind of sin is it deliberately to omit telling a mortal sin in Confession?**

A mortal sin of sacrilege. This is called making a bad Confession.

*To undo a bad Confession, you have to confess that you made a bad Confession, confess the omitted mortal sin(s), and confess any other mortal sins you have committed since then (including Communions received in the state of mortal sin).*

**21. What should you do if you forget to confess a mortal sin?**

You must tell it in your next Confession and tell the priest that you forgot it.

*But the sin is forgiven and you may receive Communion in the meantime.*

**22. What do you do if you have no mortal sins to confess?**

Tell your venial sins and/or mention some sin already told in a previous Confession.

**23. How often do you have to go to Confession?**

At least once a year (if you have committed a mortal sin).

*If you ever commit a mortal sin, say the Act of Contrition right away and go to Confession as soon as possible. If you have perfect contrition for the mortal sin and intend to confess it in Confession, God forgives you and takes away the sin right away. But you may not receive Holy Communion until you confess it in Confession.*

**24. How often does a good Catholic go to Confession?**

Once a week, if possible, but at least once a month.

*Remember that in Confession you receive grace from the Sacrament of Penance. Besides, in Confession you receive special helps to overcome the temptations that bother you most.*

## PRACTICAL POINTS

**1.** In Confession the eternal punishment (Hell) is taken away, but all of the temporal punishment due to your sins is not always taken away. "Temporal punishment" means that, even though all your sins are forgiven through the Sacrament of Penance, God still requires that you be punished for your sins, either in this life or in Purgatory. So, Confession does not make sinning easier. One of the chief ways by which you can make up for your sins is by gaining indulgences. (See Lesson 26, Pages 95-97).

**2.** If you are in danger of death and cannot go to Confession right away, be sure to make an act of perfect contrition; say the Act of Contrition, or simply tell God you are sorry for all your sins *because they offend Him,* who is all good, and beg His mercy. If somebody else (whether Catholic or not) is in danger of death, it is a great act of charity to help him to be sorry for offending God and to beg God's mercy.

# $\mathcal{L}$ελλon 25: How to Go to Confession

## 1. Examination of conscience.

Kneel in church and ask God to help you know your sins. Try to remember, as well as you can, what sins you have committed since your last Confession and how many times or how often you committed each one. Tell God that you are sorry for your sins. Then go over to the confessional booth and pray while waiting your turn to go in.

## 2. In the confessional.

Kneel down and wait until the priest opens the little window. Make the Sign of the Cross and say:

"Forgive me, Father, for I have sinned; it is one week (or one month or whatever length of time it is) since my last Confession. I accuse myself of the following sins."

Name the sins and tell how many times you committed each one. Then say:

"I am sorry for these sins and all the sins of my whole life, especially (here name some sin already confessed)."

The priest will then give you some prayers as penance, and perhaps advise you. While the priest is saying the words of forgiveness ("absolution"), you should say the *Act of Contrition*. Then the priest will say, "God bless you," or "Go in peace," or something like that. You say, "Thank you, Father," make the Sign of the Cross and go out of the confessional.

## 3. After your Confession.

Go back to your pew, kneel down, say your penance and thank God for the Sacrament of Penance.

93

## PRACTICAL POINTS

1. Remember that you can go to any priest anywhere. The priest does not know who is confessing to him. He cannot see you, and it is difficult to recognize a voice speaking in a whisper. You do not tell the priest your name or give any details that would identify you.

2. Speak to the priest in a whisper. Tell your sins briefly; do not go into detail. However, in confessing a sin of impurity, you have to tell what kind it is (thought, desire, adultery, fornication, etc.). In confessing a sin of theft, tell the amount or value of the object stolen.

3. If you are not sure whether or not you were guilty of some sin, confess the sin but tell the priest you are not sure you committed it. Example: I was tempted by impure thoughts and I may have consented to them.

4. Go to Confession often and regularly, even though you have no mortal sins to confess. You should not think of Confession as just a way of getting rid of your sins. Remember that in Confession you receive the Sacrament of Penance. This Sacrament not only gives you grace, but also helps you to overcome future temptations. It is difficult to lead a good life without going to Confession often. Go once a week if possible; once a month at the very least. (Some Saints confessed daily.)

INSIDE THE CONFESSIONAL
*The arrows indicate the heavy screen between priest and penitent.*

# *Lesson 26:* Indulgences

*"Jesus saith to them: But whom do you say that I am? Simon Peter answered and said: Thou art Christ, the Son of the living God. And Jesus answering, said to him: Blessed art thou, Simon Bar-Jona: because flesh and blood hath not revealed it to thee, but my Father who is in heaven. And I say to thee: That thou art Peter; and upon this rock I will build my church, and the gates of hell shall not prevail against it. And I will give to thee the keys of the kingdom of heaven. And whatsoever thou shalt bind upon earth, it shall be bound also in heaven: and whatsoever thou shalt loose on earth, it shall be loosed also in heaven."* (Matthew 16:15-19).

## 1. Can all your sins be forgiven in Confession?
Yes, if you are truly sorry for them.

> *"If we confess our sins, he is faithful and just, to forgive us our sins, and to cleanse us from all iniquity."* (1 John 1:9).

## 2. In Confession is all the punishment due to your sins taken away?
1) In Confession the eternal punishment (Hell) is taken away;
2) all of the temporal punishment is not always taken away.

## 3. What is meant by "temporal punishment"?
"Temporal punishment" means that, even though all your sins are forgiven in Confession, God still demands that you be punished (for a time) either in this life or in Purgatory.

## 4. What is an indulgence?
An indulgence is the taking away of all or part of the temporal punishment still due to sin.

## 5. How do indulgences take away temporal punishment?

The Church has the authority from Jesus Christ to draw on the spiritual treasury made up of the merits of Christ, His Mother and the Saints.

*"Whatsoever thou shalt loose on earth, it shall be loosed also in heaven."* (Matthew 16:19).

## 6. What do you have to do to gain an indulgence?

You have to—

1) have no mortal sin on your soul;

2) say the prayer or do the work to which the indulgence is attached;

3) have the intention of gaining the indulgence, and

4) fulfill all the conditions laid down by the Church for each indulgence.

## 7. How many kinds of indulgences are there?

Two kinds: plenary and partial.

## 8. What is a plenary indulgence?

One that takes away *all* the temporal punishment due to sin.

*Examples: saying the Rosary before the Blessed Sacrament, making the Way of the Cross, attending Forty Hours Devotion, reading the Bible as spiritual reading for at least half an hour. A person can gain only one plenary indulgence per day, except in danger of death, when he may gain a second one.*

## 9. What else is required to gain a plenary indulgence?

1) Confession (at least within several days);

2) Communion (preferably on the same day you perform the indulgenced prayer or work);

3) Prayer for the Holy Father's intentions (at least one Our Father and one Hail Mary);

4) Having no attachment in your heart to sin.

## 10. What is a partial indulgence?

One that takes away only *part* of the temporal punishment.

*Examples: using holy water, medals or statues that have been blessed, reciting the Litany of the Blessed Virgin Mary.*

## 11. Can you gain an indulgence for someone else?

Yes, for the souls in Purgatory only.

*The month of November is dedicated to the souls in Purgatory. During this month, Catholics are especially urged to gain indulgences for the Poor Souls to impress on them the importance of praying for the Poor Souls at all times.*

## 12. Can temporal punishment be taken away by any other means?

Yes, the Sacrament of Extreme Unction takes away all temporal punishment due to your sins, if you receive it with perfect intentions. Plus, any prayer or good work done in the state of grace takes away some temporal punishment, but indulgences take away more.

# Lesson 27:

## The Sacrament of Extreme Unction

*"Is any man sick among you? Let him bring in the priests of the church, and let them pray over him, anointing him with oil in the name of the Lord. And the prayer of faith shall save the sick man: and the Lord shall raise him up: and if he be in sins, they shall be forgiven him."* (James 5:13-15).

**1. What is the Sacrament of Extreme Unction?**

Extreme Unction is the Sacrament which gives health and strength to the soul and sometimes to the body to persons who are in danger of death.

> The words "extreme unction" mean "last anointing." In Baptism, Confirmation and Holy Orders, the body is anointed with holy oil. In the Sacrament of Extreme Unction the body is anointed for the last time. Hence the name.

**2. How is Extreme Unction given?**

After praying over the sick person, the priest anoints (makes the Sign of the Cross with the Holy Oil) on the person's eyes, ears, nostrils, lips, hands and feet.

**3. What does the priest say while anointing the sick person?**

He says: "Through this holy anointing, and by His most tender mercy, may the Lord pardon you what sins you have committed by sight (hearing, speech, and so on)."

**4. What does Extreme Unction do for your soul?**

The Sacrament of Extreme Unction—

1) gives you more Sanctifying Grace;

2) helps you to bear your sufferings;

3) strengthens you against the temptations of the devil;

4) sometimes gives back your health;

5) takes away temporal punishment due to sin; and

6) prepares you for immediate entry into Heaven.

## 5. Does Extreme Unction take away sin?

Extreme Unction takes away—

1) all your venial sins, and

2) even your mortal sins if you are unable to confess them but are truly sorry for them.

## 6. Who can give Extreme Unction?

Only a Catholic priest.

## 7. Who can receive Extreme Unction?

Any Catholic in danger of death from sickness, old age or accident not only can but should receive Extreme Unction.

*However, it may not be given to infants or to anyone who has never had the use of reason.*

## 8. When should you receive Extreme Unction?

Whenever the sickness or accident is so serious that it could cause death.

*Examples: pneumonia, heart attack, a serious car accident.*

## 9. How often can you receive Extreme Unction?

Only once in the same danger of death.

*However, if a new danger arises, you can receive it again.*

## 10. What should be done in case of sudden death?

Send for a priest right away, because Extreme Unction may be given even after a person is apparently dead.

*Even when a person displays all the usual manifestations of death, the soul may still not have departed from the body. Therefore, the Church allows Extreme Unction to be administered for a time after "death" has occurred.*

## 11. Why is it wrong to wait until the sick person is unconscious before sending for the priest?

Because the sick person must be conscious in order to benefit the most from the Sacrament.

## 12. What kind of sin is it to deprive a sick person of Extreme Unction?

A mortal sin.

*It often happens that a convert is the only Catholic in a family. If this is your case, therefore, you should tell your relatives to send for the priest if you are ever in danger of death.*

## 13. What should be done before the priest comes to anoint the sick person?

Spread a white cloth on a table beside the bed. Then put a crucifix, two blessed candles, a bottle of holy water, a glass of drinking water, a spoon and some cotton on the table.

*A member of the family, carrying a lighted candle, should meet the priest at the door and lead him to the sickroom. No one should talk to the priest, for he probably has the Holy Eucharist with him. Everyone should kneel down when he enters. If you do not have the above items,* call the priest anyway.

## 14. What does the priest do when he enters the sickroom?

First, he says some prayers, sprinkles the sick person with holy water and hears his Confession. Then he gives him Holy Communion and Extreme Unction, and finally, the Last Blessing.

*All of these together are called the Last Sacraments or Last Rites of the Church. (Everyone else leaves the room while the priest hears the sick person's Confession.)*

### PRACTICAL POINTS

1. Do not worry that a sick person will be frightened by the priest, because Catholics should always be glad to see the priest in order to receive the comforts that only the Sacraments can bring.

2. If you are going to be a patient in a non-Catholic hospital, tell your parish priest which one you are going to and how long you expect to be there. Also, tell the doctors and nurses that you are Catholic and that they should send for a priest if you become critical or serious.

3. Catholics should be buried in Catholic cemeteries. Tell your relatives to see your parish priest about your funeral. Or, make the arrangements yourself ahead of time.

4. Catholics have traditionally been forbidden to have their bodies cremated, except in case of a serious public necessity. The Catholic burial service has traditionally been denied those who give orders to have their bodies cremated.

# Lesson 28:

## The Sacrament of Holy Orders (Priesthood)

### JESUS CHRIST THE PRIEST

*"Having therefore a great high priest that hath passed into the heavens, Jesus the Son of God: let us hold fast our confession. For we have not a high priest, who can not have compassion on our infirmities: but one tempted in all things like as we are, without sin. Let us go therefore with confidence to the throne of grace: that we may obtain mercy, and find grace in seasonable aid. For every high priest taken from among men, is ordained for men in the things that appertain to God, that he may offer up gifts and sacrifices for sins: who can have compassion on them that are ignorant and that err: because he himself also is compassed with infirmity. And therefore he ought, as for the people, so also for himself, to offer for sins. Neither doth any man take the honour to himself, but he that is called by God, as Aaron was."* (Hebrews 4:14-16, 5:1-4).

### JESUS COMMISSIONS HIS FIRST PRIESTS

*"And Jesus coming, spoke to them, saying: All power is given to me in heaven and in earth. Going therefore, teach ye all nations; baptizing them in the name of the Father, and of the Son, and of the Holy Ghost. Teaching them to observe all things whatsoever I have commanded you: and behold I am with you all days, even to the consummation of the world."* (Matthew 28:18-20).

1. **What did Jesus do to continue His work on earth?**

   To make sure that His work would be continued, Jesus established the Catholic Priesthood, through the Sacrament of Holy Orders.

   *"For Christ therefore we are ambassadors, God as it were exhorting by us."* (2 Corinthians 5:20).

## 2. What is the Sacrament of Holy Orders?

Holy Orders is the Sacrament which gives a man the powers of the Catholic Priesthood.

## 3. In general, what is a priest?

A man who offers sacrifice to God for the sins of the people.

*"For every high priest taken from among men, is ordained for men in the things that appertain to God, that he may offer up gifts and sacrifices for sins."* (Hebrews 5:1).

## 4. Was Jesus a priest?

Yes, Jesus was and is the Great High Priest.

*"Wherefore it behoved him in all things to be made like unto his brethren, that he might become a merciful and faithful high priest before God, that he might be a propitiation for the sins of the people."* (Hebrews 2:17).

## 5. Who were the first Catholic priests?

The twelve Apostles, who were ordained to the priesthood by Jesus Christ Himself.

## 6. When did Jesus make the twelve Apostles priests?

At the Last Supper, on the night before He died, when He gave them the power to change bread and wine into His Body and Blood.

*"Do this for a commemoration of me."* (Luke 22:19).

## 7. Did the Apostles make other men priests?

Yes, for example, Paul, Barnabas, Timothy, Titus and Matthias.

*See Acts 13:3, 14:22, 1:24-26 and Titus 1:5.*

## 8. How did the Apostles ordain other men priests?

By praying for them and imposing hands on them.

*"Then they, fasting and praying, and imposing their hands upon them, sent them away."* (Acts 13:3).

**9. After the Apostles died, how were the powers of the priesthood handed down?**

Before they died, the Apostles made other men bishops, who in turn made other men bishops, and in this way the powers of the priesthood have been handed down during the past 2000 years.

**10. How are the powers of the priesthood handed down today?**

Today the bishops hand down the powers of the priesthood just as the Apostles did—by praying over and imposing hands on the candidates for priesthood.

**11. What are the chief powers of the priesthood?**

They are—

1) to offer the Holy Sacrifice of the Mass, which includes the power to change bread and wine into the Body and Blood of Jesus Christ; and

2) to forgive sins.

*Other powers of the priesthood are to preach with authority, administer other Sacraments and to bless people and objects.*

**12. Where does the authority of the priesthood come from?**

From Jesus Christ, the Second Person of the Holy Trinity.

*"He that heareth you, heareth me; and he that despiseth you, despiseth me; and he that despiseth me, despiseth him that sent me."* (Luke 10:16).

**13. Who can give the Sacrament of Holy Orders?**

Only a bishop.

*"For this cause I left thee in Crete, that thou shouldest set in order the things that are wanting, and shouldest ordain priests in every city, as I also appointed thee."* (Titus 1:5).

**14. What is necessary to become a priest?**

To become a priest, a man has to study for about 12 years in a special school called a seminary and be approved by his bishop as to his learning, health, morals and character.

*"Impose not hands lightly upon any man."* (1 Timothy 5:22).

**15. How does a man become a bishop?**

The Pope chooses a priest who is known for his learning and holiness and appoints other bishops to consecrate him a bishop by imposing hands and saying the proper words.

**16. How does a man become Pope?**

The Cardinals elect a successor to the dead Pope.

**17. Why do priests not get married?**

They do not marry because—

1) the single life is a holier life, recommended by Christ;

2) being single, they can give themselves entirely to God and the care of the people.

*"He that is without a wife, is solicitous for the things that belong to the Lord, how he may please God. But he that is with a wife, is solicitous for the things of the world, how he may please his wife: and he is divided."* (1 Corinthians 7:32-33).

**18. Why is the priest called "Father"?**

Because he gives the life of grace to his spiritual children, just as a father gives physical life to his children.

*"I write not these things to confound you; but I admonish you as my dearest children. For if you have ten thousand instructors in Christ, yet not many fathers. For in Christ Jesus, by the gospel, I have begotten you."* (1 Corinthians 4:14-15).

### VARIOUS TITLES IN THE CHURCH

Pope:     The bishop of Rome, vicar of Christ on earth, successor of St. Peter, visible head of the whole Catholic Church.

Cardinal:     An honorary title given to priests or bishops because of their important positions in the Church; Cardinals elect the new Pope.

Bishop:     Rules over the people and priests of his diocese; can give Confirmation and Holy Orders.

Monsignor:     A priest gets this honorary title from the Pope because of his important position in the Church.

| Pastor: | Rules over a parish; is subject to the bishop of the diocese. |
|---|---|
| Priest: | Diocesan priests work in a diocese; religious priests belong to a religious order—like the Franciscans, Dominicans, etc. |
| Monk: | Monks live in a monastery, follow a strict rule under a superior—like the Benedictines and the Trappists; some are priests, others are brothers. |
| Brother: | A man dedicated to teaching, hospital work or contemplation; takes vows of poverty, chastity and obedience, but does not receive the Sacrament of Holy Orders. |
| Sister: | A woman dedicated to teaching, hospital or social work, or contemplation; takes vows of poverty, chastity and obedience and belongs to a religious order or community. Cloistered sisters are usually called nuns; loosely speaking, all sisters are often called nuns. |

# $\mathcal{L}\varepsilon\delta\delta on$ 29: The Nature of Marriage

## GOD MADE MARRIAGE

*"And God created man to his own image: to the image of God he created him: male and female he created them. And God blessed them, saying: Increase and multiply, and fill the earth, and subdue it."* (Genesis 1:27-28).

**1. Who made marriage?**

God made marriage and the laws concerning marriage.

**2. When did God make marriage?**

When He created Adam and Eve.

**3. Why did God make marriage?**

For two purposes:

1) for bringing children into the world and raising them, and

2) for the mutual help of husband and wife.

**4. How do you know that the first purpose of marriage is children?**

The Bible says so—"Increase and multiply." (*Genesis* 1:28).

> *"I will therefore that the younger should marry, bear children, be mistresses of families."* (1 Timothy 5:14).

**5. Does not common sense show that the first purpose of marriage is children?**

Yes, the very differences, both physical and mental, between man and woman show the first purpose of marriage to be the bringing of children into the world.

> *A woman's body is made for the bearing and nursing of children; whereas, a man's body is stronger so that he can protect his family and give them food and shelter. A woman is kinder, more sympathetic, more emotional than man. She needs these qualities to care for and instruct her children.*

**107**

### 6. How do you know that mutual love and help are the second purpose of marriage?

The Bible says so:

*"And the Lord God said: It is not good for man to be alone: let us make him a help like unto him self...Then the Lord God cast a deep sleep upon Adam: and when he was fast asleep, he took one of his ribs, and filled up flesh for it. And the Lord God built the rib which he took from Adam into a woman: and brought her to Adam."* (Genesis 2:18,21-22).

### 7. Does not common sense indicate this too?

Yes, common sense shows that men and women are incomplete without one another but find their physical and spiritual completion in marriage.

*A man needs the sympathy, understanding and encouragement of a wife, while the wife needs his love, affection, direction and companionship.*

### 8. What is the purpose of sexual pleasure?

To attract husband and wife to have children and to foster love for each other.

### 9. Who are the only ones that may enjoy sexual pleasure?

Husband and wife who are validly married to each other.

*"But I say to the unmarried, and to the widows: It is good for them if they so continue, even as I. But if they do not contain themselves, let them marry. For it is better to marry than to be burnt."* (1 Corinthians 7:8-9).

### 10. How many wives did God create for Adam?

Only one wife; God wanted this marriage to be the model for all marriages—one man and one woman.

*"Wherefore a man shall leave father and mother, and shall cleave to his wife: and they shall be two in one flesh."* (Genesis 2:24).

### 11. How long does God intend husband and wife to stay together?

Until the death of one of the partners.

*"A woman is bound by the law as long as her husband liveth; but if her husband die, she is at liberty: let her marry to whom she will; only in the Lord."* (1 Corinthians 7:39).

**12. Why does God command husband and wife to stay together until death?**

Because the lifetime welfare of the children and of the married couple themselves requires that they be permanently united.

*Divine law requires the couple to stay together until death, even if they have no children. In special cases separation is permitted, but the bond of marriage remains.*

**13. What is a valid marriage?**

A union that is a real marriage in the eyes of God and therefore can be broken only by death.

*No power on earth, therefore, can break a valid marriage. "What therefore God hath joined together, let not man put asunder." (Mark 10:9). This includes the State (the civil government).*

**14. What Is an invalid marriage?**

A union that never was a marriage in the eyes of God.

*A couple invalidly married must either separate or have the marriage made valid. Otherwise they are living in adultery or fornication. "Neither fornicators...nor adulterers...shall possess the kingdom of God." (1 Corinthians 6:9-10).*

**15. What is necessary for a valid marriage?**

1) A single man and a single woman, 2) who are of age, 3) free to marry, 4) capable of sexual intercourse, 5) who intend to live together, 6) to be faithful to each other until the death of one of them, 7) who intend to have a family, and 8) who are in no other way prohibited by the law of God from marrying.

*For example, it is forbidden to marry close relatives, such as uncles, aunts, nieces or nephews.*

**16. Did God make these laws only for Catholics?**

No, all human beings have to obey these laws.

*However, Catholics are also bound by Church laws. For example, a Catholic cannot marry validly except in the presence of a priest and two witnesses (unless there is a special dispensation from the local bishop for a particular case and that for a sufficiently grave reason).*

**17. Does the state have authority to change God's laws?**

No. God's law comes before man's law.

*But, the State (civil government) can make laws requiring a license and registration, and concerning health, property rights, and so on, as long as these laws are not against God's laws.*

**18. Can men and women find real happiness in marriage?**

Yes, if they follow God's plan for marriage.

*"Happy is the husband of a good wife: for the number of his years is double. A virtuous woman rejoiceth her husband and shall fulfil the years of his life in peace. A good wife is a good portion, she shall be given in the portion of them that fear God, to a man for his good deeds. Rich or poor, if his heart is good, his countenance shall be cheerful at all times."* (Ecclesiasticus 26:1-4).

**19. What is the greatest source of happiness in marriage?**

Raising children in the fear and love of God.

*Court records show fewer marriage breakups among couples with large families.*

## PRACTICAL POINTS

1. All laws, both human and divine, are made for the good of society. Once in a while, a law will work a hardship on an individual, and this is sometimes true of God's laws on marriage. But you marry "for better or for worse." Therefore, if through no fault of yours, your married life is unhappy, or if your partner has left you, or if you find God's laws hard to observe, ask God for the strength to do His will; ask your crucified Saviour for the courage to carry your cross. The Sacrament of Matrimony gives married people special graces to live their lives according to God's laws. In any case, God made no exceptions to His laws on marriage; to break them for any reason is a serious sin.

2. Do not try to judge whether your marriage or anybody else's is valid or invalid. That can be done only by one who is skilled in the knowledge of these laws. The priest who is instructing you will tell you whether your marriage is valid or not.

**3.** An "annulment" is not the dissolving of an existing marriage, but rather a declaration that a real marriage never existed in the eyes of God on account of some dire defect or impediment that was present *at the time the couple exchanged their vows.* For example, if one of the two parties did not intend to enter a permanent union until death, no marriage would take place, despite the appearances. An annulment is more properly termed a "declaration of nullity."

# Lesson 30:
## The Sins Against Marriage

### SEPARATION AND REFUSING THE MARRIAGE DEBT

*"But for fear of fornication, let every man have his own wife, and let every woman have her own husband. Let the husband render the debt to his wife, and the wife also in like manner to the husband. The wife hath not power of her own body, but the husband. And in like manner the husband also hath not power of his own body, but the wife. Defraud not one another, except, perhaps, by consent, for a time, that you may give yourselves to prayer; and return together again, lest Satan tempt you for your incontinency."* (1 Corinthians 7:2-5).

### DIVORCE

*"And the Pharisees coming to him asked him: Is it lawful for a man to put away his wife? tempting him. But he answering, saith to them: What did Moses command you? Who said: Moses permitted to write a bill of divorce, and to put her away. To whom Jesus answering, said: Because of the hardness of your heart he wrote you that precept. But from the beginning of the creation, God made them male and female. For this cause a man shall leave his father and mother; and shall cleave to his wife. And they two shall be in one flesh. Therefore now they are not two, but one flesh. What therefore God hath joined together, let not man put asunder. And in the house again his disciples asked him concerning the same thing. And he saith to them: Whosoever shall put away his wife and marry another, committeth adultery against her. And if the wife shall put away her husband, and be married to another, she committeth adultery."* (Mark 10:2-12).

112

## BIRTH CONTROL

*"Juda therefore said to Onan his son: Go in to thy [deceased] brother's wife and marry her, that thou mayst raise seed to thy brother.* He knowing *that the children should not be his, when he went in to his brother's wife, spilled* his seed upon the ground, lest children should be born in his brother's name. And therefore the Lord slew him, because he did a detestable thing." (Genesis 38:8-10).

**1. What are the sins against marriage?**

1) Refusing the marriage debt.

2) Unlawful separation.

3) Divorce.

4) Sinful company keeping.

5) Adultery.

6) Birth control.

7) Abortion.

8) Sterilization.

**2. What is the marriage debt?**

The "marriage debt" means that a married person is obliged, under penalty of mortal sin, to give his (or her) married partner sexual intercourse whenever it is reasonably asked for.

*Lawful excuses for refusing: adultery, sickness, drunkenness, insanity, non-support, danger to an unborn baby.*

**3. Should a married person always insist on the right to intercourse?**

No, because a marriage cannot be successful unless it is founded on love and unselfishness.

**4. Why is it a mortal sin to separate from your partner?**

Separation in a *valid* marriage is a mortal sin because—

1) God said so.

2) To separate means to refuse the marriage debt (mortal sin).

**113**

3) A separated person is tempted to commit adultery or some other sin of sex.

4) Children cannot be properly trained.

**5. Is a validly married person ever allowed to separate from his (her) spouse?**

Yes, but only for a very serious reason, and only with permission of the bishop.

**6. Why is divorce and remarriage a mortal sin?**

Because it is clearly against the law of God.

*"Every one that putteth away his wife, and marrieth another, committeth adultery: and he that marrieth her that is put away from her husband, committeth adultery." (Luke 16:18). "A woman is bound by the law as long as her husband liveth; but if her husband die, she is at liberty: let her marry to whom she will; only in the Lord." (1 Corinthians 7:39).*

**7. May a separated or divorced person keep company with another?**

No, not if the marriage is valid, because such a person is still married, and a married person is never allowed to keep company with another.

*"Therefore while her husband liveth, she shall be called an adulteress, if she be with another man." (Romans 7:3).*

**8. What is adultery?**

Sexual intercourse between a married person and someone to whom he (or she) is not married.

**9. What is the sin of birth control?**

Doing anything before, during or after intercourse to keep the woman from becoming pregnant.

*"Marriage honourable in all, and the marriage bed undefiled." (Hebrews 13:4). "He [Onan]...when he went in to his [deceased] brother's wife, spilled his seed upon the ground, lest children should be born in his brother's name. And therefore the Lord slew him, because he did a detestable thing." (Genesis 38:9-10).*

## 10. Is birth control ever allowed by God?

No, it is *always* a mortal sin.

*"He [Onan]. . .when he went in to his [deceased] brother's wife, spilled his seed upon the ground, lest children should be born in his brother's name. And therefore the Lord slew him, because he did a detestable thing."* (Genesis 38:9-10).

## 11. What is the sin of abortion?

Killing an unborn baby.

*"Thou shalt not kill."* (Fifth Commandment).

## 12. Is abortion ever allowed to save a mother's life?

No, because to take away the life of any innocent human being, even that of an unborn human being, is always murder.

*From just the medical point of view, abortion is not the safe and simple procedure it is made out to be. It can cause serious injury to the woman, and even death. Women who have had abortions become sterile and miscarry more often than those who have not, plus abortion leads more often to tubal pregnancies than in women who have not aborted their children. Doctors concede that it is always safer for the woman to come to term with her pregnancy than to have an abortion, even if this means having a caesarian.*

## 13. What happens to a Catholic who knowingly has an abortion?

Automatic excommunication is the penalty for this crime.

*This means that such a person cannot receive the Sacraments nor have a Catholic funeral.*

## 14. Can an excommunicated person get back into the Church?

Yes, if he is truly sorry for having committed the crime.

*However, the priest who hears his confession has to get special power from the bishop to take away the excommunication.*

## 15. What is sterilization?

Making the reproductive organs unfruitful, usually by tying or cutting the Fallopian tubes, cutting or tying the seminal vesicles (vasectomy), or removing the ovaries or uterus (hysterectomy).

## 16. What kind of sin is sterilization?

Always a mortal sin, unless the organs are diseased and must be removed because they are a danger to the health of the whole body.

*A woman is never allowed to have her tubes tied nor a man allowed to have a vasectomy under any conditions, even under doctors' orders. If there is serious danger to the woman's life or health, the only solution in accord with God's law is to refrain from sexual intercourse totally or periodically. (See Point 3 below).*

### PRACTICAL POINTS

1. The sins discussed in this lesson are against the law of God and are therefore forbidden to everyone, not just to Catholics.

2. If lack of money or poor health make it difficult for you to have children, consider that this is the cross Jesus wants you to carry and that He will give you the strength to carry it.

3. For a truly serious reason (for example, if the mother's life would be endangered by pregnancy), it is not against God's law for a couple to practice periodic continence—that is, to have sexual intercourse only during the woman's infertile time each month. This practice is allowed only 1) with mutual consent, 2) if it is not an occasion of sin, and 3) for a sufficiently grave reason. The practice must not be continued any longer than necessary.

4. Expectant mothers should be careful about signing papers in the hospital; they should not consent to a D & C unless it is certain the baby is already dead.

5. Women having abdominal operations should tell the doctor not to tie the tubes. (A woman who has had her tubes tied is not required to have them untied. However, to do so is praiseworthy and proves the woman has true contrition for having had her tubes tied.)

6. Birth control pills often work by causing early abortion. The IUD is an abortifacient also.

# *Lesson 31:*
## The Sacrament of Matrimony

*"Being subject one to another, in the fear of Christ. Let women be subject to their husbands, as to the Lord: Because the husband is the head of the wife, as Christ is the head of the church. He is the saviour of his body. Therefore as the church is subject to Christ, so also let the wives be to their husbands in all things.*

*"Husbands, love your wives, as Christ also loved the church, and delivered himself up for it: That he might sanctify it, cleansing it by the laver of water in the word of life: That he might present it to himself a glorious church, not having spot or wrinkle, or any such thing; but that it should be holy, and without blemish. So also ought men to love their wives as their own bodies. He that loveth his wife, loveth himself. For no man ever hated his own flesh; but nourisheth and cherisheth it, as also Christ doth the church: Because we are members of his body, of his flesh, and of his bones. For this cause shall a man leave his father and mother, and shall cleave to his wife, and they shall be two in one flesh. This is a great sacrament; but I speak in Christ and in the church.*

*"Nevertheless let every one of you in particular love his wife as himself: and let the wife fear her husband."* (Ephesians 5:21-33).

### 1. What is the Sacrament of Matrimony?
Matrimony is the Sacrament made by Jesus Christ to sanctify (make holy) the lawful union of a Christian man and a Christian woman.

### 2. Was marriage always a Sacrament?
No, marriage, although always a sacred union of man and woman, was raised to the dignity of a Sacrament by Jesus Christ.

**117**

**3. What does this Sacrament do for a couple?**

1) It unites them in an indissoluble (unbreakable) union until death;

2) it makes Sanctifying Grace grow in their souls;

3) it gives them special helps to perform their duties as married people and to overcome the difficulties that may come into their married life.

**4. Who may receive the Sacrament of Matrimony?**

Only those who have been baptized and are free to marry.

**5. What is necessary to receive this Sacrament worthily?**

You have to be free of mortal sin.

**6. What kind of sin is it to receive this Sacrament unworthily?**

A mortal sin of sacrilege.

*However, the marriage is valid.*

**7. Do Catholics have to be married at Mass?**

No, but it is certainly fitting that they do so.

*The special Mass for a Catholic wedding is called the Nuptial Mass. Traditionally, this Mass was not celebrated for a mixed marriage, nor during Lent or Advent. But now it may be celebrated, if the couple desires it. Also, it can now be said during Lent and Advent, save from Holy Thursday through Easter Sunday.*

**8. What should a Catholic do who wants to marry?**

Preparations for the wedding should be made with one of the priests in the bride's parish several months in advance.

*This time requirement varies from diocese to diocese.*

**9. What is the only way a Catholic can be married?**

Only in the presence of a Catholic priest and two witnesses.

*Occasionally other arrangements can be made, but this requires a dispensation in advance from the local bishop and can be done only for a sufficiently grave reason.*

**10. What happens if a Catholic is not married by a priest?**

A Catholic who goes through a marriage ceremony before anyone other than a Catholic priest is not married.

*Such a couple has to separate or have the marriage made valid.*

**11. What if a Catholic goes through a marriage ceremony before a Protestant minister?**

Such a person is not married and is guilty of mortal sin.

*Traditionally this sin also carried the penalty of automatic excommunication. This meant that such a person could not receive any of the Sacraments nor have a Catholic funeral. However, although this penalty no longer applies, a Catholic who goes through a marriage ceremony outside the Catholic Church still commits a grave sin.*

**12. May a Catholic marry a non-Catholic?**

No, except for a very serious reason.

*A marriage between a Catholic and a non-Catholic is called a mixed marriage.*

**13. Why does the Church forbid mixed marriages?**

Because of the danger of loss of faith on the part of the Catholic and of the children.

*The different religious beliefs of the parents cause serious arguments on such important matters as divorce, birth control, Sunday Mass, eating meat on Friday and the Catholic education of the children.*

**14. Were mixed marriages forbidden in the Bible?**

Yes, mixed marriages were strictly forbidden by God.

*"Neither shalt thou make marriages with them. Thou shalt not give thy daughter to his son, nor take his daughter for thy son: For she will turn away thy son from following me, that he may rather serve strange gods, and the wrath of the Lord will be kindled, and will quickly destroy thee." (Deuteronomy 7:3-4).*

**15. Who is the only one who can allow a mixed marriage?**

Only the bishop, and he can give permission only for a serious reason.

**16. In a mixed marriage, what must the Catholic promise?**

The Catholic must sign promises: 1) to remain a Catholic and 2) to see to it that the children are baptized and are brought up as Catholics. Also, the Catholic party must inform the non-Catholic of these promises.

## 17. Are the marriages of non-Catholics valid?

Yes, provided all the laws of God concerning marriage are observed, the marriages of non-Catholics among themselves are valid and therefore cannot be broken.

## PRACTICAL POINTS

1. It is not the priest who gives the Sacrament of Matrimony; he is only the chief witness. The bride and groom give it to each other. The first gift they give one another is an increase of God's life—Sanctifying Grace. It is fitting indeed that this giving be done at Mass.

2. Couples should remember that, through the Sacrament of Matrimony, they have the right to special helps to aid them in their problems. God gives them, as it were, a spiritual bank account on which they may draw in times of difficulty.

3. In a mixed marriage, the non-Catholic should be encouraged to take a course of instructions, so that he (or she) may learn something about the Catholic religion, since the children have to be raised in the Catholic religion. So, if you intend to marry a non-Catholic, bring him (or her) to the priest to begin instructions three or four months before the wedding.

4. Under normal circumstances, a mixed marriage can take place only in the presence of a Catholic priest and two witnesses.

5. Non-Catholics can marry validly in the presence of anyone who can perform marriages legally (minister, rabbi, judge, justice of the peace, captain of a ship).

6. A Catholic may act as best man or bridesmaid at a wedding that takes place in a non-Catholic church only if it is a *valid* marriage.

# *Lesson 32:*
## How to Have a Happy Marriage

*"Then Tobias exhorted the virgin, and said to her: Sara, arise, and let us pray to God today, and tomorrow, and the next day: because for these three nights we are joined to God: and when the third night is over, we will be in our own wedlock. For we are the children of saints, and we must not be joined together like heathens that know not God. So they both arose, and prayed earnestly both together that health might be given them, and Tobias said: Lord God of our fathers, may the heavens and the earth, and the sea, and the fountains, and the rivers, and all thy creatures that are in them, bless thee. Thou madest Adam of the slime of the earth, and gavest him Eve for a helper. And now, Lord, thou knowest, that not for fleshly lust do I take my sister to wife, but only for the love of posterity, in which thy name may be blessed for ever and ever. Sara also said: Have mercy on us, O Lord, have mercy on us, and let us grow old both together in health."* (Tobias 8:4-10).

### 1. Have the correct attitude.

Look upon marriage as a very holy union, founded by God and raised to the dignity of a Sacrament by Jesus Christ as a means of saving your soul.

### 2. Have the correct purpose.

Look forward to having children and founding a Christian home.

> People who marry for selfish reasons (money, pleasure, beauty, fame, influence) very seldom, if ever, find happiness in marriage.

### 3. Do not marry for selfish reasons.

Genuine happiness is attained only by those who are completely generous and ready to sacrifice themselves in all things.

**121**

### 4. Study what marriage is.

Marriage, like a career, requires specialized knowledge, and this is obtained through study and prayer.

*Receive marriage instructions from a priest and/or read about the duties and graces of Catholic marriage (such as are explained in this book).*

### 5. Pray for a happy marriage.

You should pray every day for a happy marriage, because most probably you will save your soul or lose your soul as a married person.

*"House and riches are given by parents: but a prudent wife is properly from the Lord." (Proverbs 19:14).*

### 6. Prepare for marriage by living a Christian life.

Receive Holy Communion worthily and often; go to Confession regularly; observe the Ten Commandments, especially the 6th.

### 7. Follow the advice of your parents and your parish priest.

It is wise to seek advice when making any important decision, but especially when deciding about your partner in this lifelong union.

### 8. Choose a suitable partner.

Look for a person who is a good Catholic, really serious about having children and founding a Christian home, one who is sincere, truthful, dependable and chaste.

### 9. Do not marry too young.

Today, young people under twenty-one (especially young men), although capable of marrying and having children, are often still attached to youthful pastimes and thus may find it extra difficult to adjust to the responsibilities of marriage.

## 10. Have the correct attitude toward sex.

God created sex to attract husband and wife to have children and to cultivate love for one another.

*Remember—to refuse intercourse to your married partner is a mortal sin, unless you have a serious reason.*

## 11. Accept all the children that God wants to send you.

Look upon having children as one of the great blessings of marriage.

*Court records show that there are fewer breakups among couples with large families.*

## 12. Have respect for your partner.

The person you marry shares in a union that was established by God Himself and raised to the dignity of a Sacrament by Christ.

*"Ye husbands, likewise dwelling with them according to knowledge, giving honour to the female as to the weaker vessel, and as to the co-heirs of the grace of life: that your prayers be not hindered." (1 Peter 3:7).*

## 13. Do not fight or argue!

Married people should learn to control their tempers and to discuss their problems as grown-ups and not as children.

*"Bearing with one another, and forgiving one another, if any have a complaint against another: even as the Lord hath forgiven you, so do you also. But above all these things have charity, which is the bond of perfection: And let the peace of Christ rejoice in your hearts, wherein also you are called in one body: and be ye thankful...Wives, be subject to your husbands, as it behoveth in the Lord. Husbands, love your wives, and be not bitter towards them." (Colossians 3:13-15, 18-19).*

## 14. Do not criticize!

Criticizing your partner's faults or constantly harping on trifles soon destroys a happy marriage.

*"And why seest thou the mote [speck] that is in thy brother's eye; and seest not the beam that is in thy own eye? Or how sayest thou to thy brother: Let me cast the mote out of thy eye; and behold a beam is in thy own eye?" (Matthew 7:3-4).*

### 15. Trust one another completely.

It is a sin to be jealous or judge without evidence.

*"Judge not, that you may not be judged. For with what judgment you judge, you shall be judged: and with what measure you mete [measure], it shall be measured to you again."* (Matthew 7:1-2).

### 16. Do not live with in-laws!

Your first duty is to your married partner; parents and others come second.

*"Wherefore a man shall leave father and mother, and shall cleave to his wife: and they shall be two in one flesh."* (Genesis 2:24).

### 17. Do things together.

Husband and wife should find happiness in their own home with their children, and also should associate with other happily married couples.

### 18. Make your home a pleasant place.

The wife should make the home a place to which her husband longs to go after his day's work; it should be clean and orderly, and the meals well prepared and on time.

*"Happy is the husband of a good wife: for the number of his years is double. A virtuous woman rejoiceth her husband and shall fulfil the years of his life in peace. A good wife is a good portion, she shall be given in the portion of them that fear God, to a man for his good deeds. Rich or poor, if his heart is good, his countenance shall be cheerful at all times."* (Ecclesiasticus 26:1-4).

### 19. Use family money properly.

A husband is bound to the complete support of his wife and children; a wife is obliged to use the family money wisely.

*"But if any man have not care of his own, and especially of those of his house, he hath denied the faith, and is worse than an infidel."* (1 Timothy 5:8).

### 20. Pray together!

As the saying goes, "A family that prays together stays together," and this includes the family Rosary, attending Mass and receiving Holy Communion together.

*"Where there are two or three gathered together in my name, there am I in the midst of them."* (Matthew 18:20).

# Lesson 33:
## Duties of Parents Toward Their Children

*"But he that shall scandalize one of these little ones that believe in me, it were better for him that a millstone should be hanged about his neck, and that he should be drowned in the depth of the sea."* (Matthew 18:6).

1. **To give their children the necessary food, clothing and shelter.**

   This obligation rests on *both* parents, whether living together or separated. They must also keep their children from all danger to life or health.

2. **To give them good example.**

   Parents give good example by observing strictly all of their religious duties, for example, of attending Mass, not eating meat on days of abstinence, carefully avoiding indecent speech, lying, cursing, criticism of others, immodesty and drunkenness.

   *Parents should remember that children are great imitators, and they should be very careful of everything they do and say in the presence of their children.*

3. **To provide a truly Catholic home for them.**

   A Catholic home is one in which God and Religion are of the greatest importance.

   *In the home there should be crucifixes, pictures of Jesus, the Blessed Virgin Mary and the Saints. Indecent pictures and calendars, sexy and sensational magazines, books, comic books, T.V. shows and videos have no place in the Christian home. There should be good books, Catholic newspapers and Catholic magazines.*

## 4. To have them baptized as soon as possible after birth.

It is a serious sin to delay the Baptism of infants, and if there is any danger to the life of the newly born baby, the priest should be called immediately.

*In danger of death, and if no priest is available, Baptism can and should be given by anyone (preferably someone other than the parents). The one baptizing need not be Catholic; he may be of any religion or of no religion. But he must have the intention of doing what the Church does in Baptism. The procedure is: Pour water over the head of the child, saying at the same time: "I baptize thee in the name of the Father and of the Son and of the Holy Ghost." For instructions on how to baptize an embryo or fetus after a miscarriage, see page 72.*

## 5. To see that they go to Confession, receive Holy Communion and receive Confirmation.

The children should be taught to go to Confession and Holy Communion regularly and frequently—every week, if possible, especially during vacation time.

## 6. To teach them to pray.

Daily prayers should be said together by the whole family.

*As the saying goes, "The family that prays together stays together." The daily family Rosary will go a very long way toward insuring that the children grow up to be good Catholics.*

## 7. To see that they go to Mass every Sunday and on the six Holy Days.

Parents should not keep children home from Mass except for very serious reasons.

## 8. To see that on Ash Wednesday and the Fridays of Lent they abstain from meat altogether, and that on the other Fridays of the year they either abstain from meat or perform a comparable penance.

See Lesson 43, page 157, especially Question 11.

## 9. To send them to a Catholic school.

This includes high school and college, as well as grammar school. Parents are forbidden by Church Law to send their children to any other kind of school.

*In very many cases today, the only truly Catholic school available is home schooling. Experience has shown that Catholic home schooling produces excellent results both spiritually and academically and that it brings great blessings to the family.*

## 10. To insist that they marry in the Catholic Church.

A Catholic *cannot* marry except in the presence of a Catholic priest and two witnesses.

*When a son or daughter begins to think seriously of marrying, the parents should have him (or her) see the priest and receive the necessary instructions on marriage. They should encourage dating only with Catholics, or at least with non-Catholics who are willing to take a full course of instructions in the Catholic Religion. Parents commit a mortal sin by forcing or unduly persuading any of their children to marry.*

## 11. To give them the Christian attitude on marriage and having children.

Parents should avoid complaining about the hardships of married life and joking about the sacred duties of marriage.

*The birth of another child should be a joyful occasion for the whole family so that the other children will consider having children as the greatest blessing of married life.*

## 12. To prepare them for marriage.

The children should be taught the serious duties and responsibilities of marriage, both by word and example.

*They should also be taught the practical side of making a home, such as cleaning, cooking, sewing, repairing, caring for children, being on time, and being neat and orderly.*

## 13. To teach them the facts on sex.

This information should be given carefully and with great emphasis on the beauty and sacredness of sex.

*Answers to questions about the facts of life should be correct, but always suited to the age and mental development of the child. Parents should encourage the confidence of their children so that the children will come to them for information.*

**14. To protect them from sin, particularly sins of impurity.**

In addition to protecting their children from bad companions, etc., parents have a grave obligation to do whatever is necessary to protect their children from classroom "Sex Education" either in public or Catholic schools.

*Formal "Sex Education" is always grossly immodest and a temptation to sin, even aside from the un-Catholic and un-Christian "slant" with which it is usually delivered.*

**15. To correct their sins and faults.**

It is a serious sin to neglect this duty.

**16. To teach them the virtues of honesty, obedience, truthfulness, purity, and modesty in dress.**

These lessons must be given early and repeated continually.

**17. To teach them respect for the rights and property of others.**

Many parents sin seriously by bad example in this matter.

**18. To teach them respect for all lawful authority.**

Children should be taught early to respect all lawful authority, especially the authority of the Church, the State and the School.

**19. To give them wholesome recreation and keep them from evil companions.**

The Christian home should be the center of the child's social life, a place where he feels free to bring his companions.

*Parents should be extremely careful about allowing their children to attend motion pictures; they should also examine their comic books and govern their use of the radio and television, as well as the VCR. Children receive many un-Christian ideas on life, marriage, crime, drinking, etc. from these sources of entertainment.*

**20. To encourage a child's desire to be a priest, a brother or a sister.**

Having a priest, brother or sister in the family is one of the greatest blessings that God can give a mother and father. Instead of turning a child away from such a desire, parents should encourage the child.

# THE 10 COMMANDMENTS

(Exodus 20:1-17)

1st. *I am the Lord thy God. Thou shalt not have strange gods before Me.*

2nd. *Thou shalt not take the name of the Lord thy God in vain.*

3rd. *Remember thou keep holy the Sabbath Day.*

4th. *Honor thy father and thy mother.*

5th. *Thou shalt not kill.*

6th. *Thou shalt not commit adultery.*

7th. *Thou shalt not steal.*

8th. *Thou shalt not bear false witness against thy neighbor.*

9th. *Thou shalt not covet thy neighbor's wife.*

10th. *Thou shalt not covet thy neighbor's goods.*

In studying the Ten Commandments, keep in mind the reason why God created you—to share in His happiness in Heaven. God gave the Ten Commandments, not to make life difficult for you, but to help you get to Heaven. "If thou wilt enter into life, keep the commandments." (*Matthew* 19:17). The Ten Commandments are another indication of God's great love for you.

# *Lesson 34:* The First Commandment

*"Come let us praise the Lord with joy: let us joyfully sing to God our saviour. Let us come before his presence with thanksgiving; and make a joyful noise to him with psalms. For the Lord is a great God, and a great King above all gods. For in his hand are all the ends of the earth: and the heights of the mountains are his. For the sea is his, and he made it: and his hands formed the dry land. Come let us adore and fall down: and weep before the Lord that made us. For he is the Lord our God: and we are the people of his pasture and the sheep of his hand."* (Psalm 94:1-7).

### 1. What is the First Commandment?

I am the Lord thy God; thou shalt not have strange gods before Me.

### 2. What does the First Commandment oblige you to do?

To offer true worship to God.

*"Adore ye him that made heaven and earth, the sea, and the fountains of waters."* (Apocalypse 14:7).

### 3. What is worship?

Acknowledging the fact that God is the Supreme Being, that He created you and that you depend entirely on Him.

*"For in him we live, and move, and are."* (Acts 17:28).

### 4. How do you worship God?

By praying to Him both in private and in public.

*"And they were always in the temple, praising and blessing God."* (Luke 24:53).

### 5. How do many people sin against the First Commandment?

By never, or at least seldom, giving worship to God.

*Very few people deny that God exists, but many live as though there were no God.*

131

### 6. What is the true worship of God?

Catholic worship, since God Himself established the Catholic Church. This includes especially the Holy Sacrifice of the Mass.

*Before Christ, the Jewish religion was the only one established by God, but it is no longer the true religion, since "in saying a new [covenant], he hath made the former old." (Hebrews 8:13).*

### 7. Name some mortal sins against the First Commandment.

1) Taking an active part in the services of a non-Catholic church.

2) Quitting the Catholic Church.

3) Joining a non-Catholic church.

4) Denying anything taught by the Catholic Church.

5) Joining the Masons or any society forbidden by the Church.

6) Joining the Communists.

7) Guiding your life by fortune telling, palmistry, phrenology, crystal gazing, horoscopes, dreams, etc.

8) Using the ouija board or practicing spiritualism.

9) Superstition, guiding your life by lucky charms, etc.

10) Reading the literature of false (that is to say, non-Catholic) religions.

### 8. Are you ever allowed to go to a non-Catholic church?

Yes, but only for the wedding or funeral of a close relative or friend or of a public official.

### 9. Are you ever allowed to take part in the religious services of a non-Catholic church?

No; this includes singing hymns or praying aloud with the congregation.

*Also, you are forbidden to act as best man or bridesmaid at a wedding at which a non-Catholic minister or rabbi officiates if the wedding is invalid.*

**10. Why does the Church condemn Masonry?**

Because Masonry is not only a secret fraternal organization but also a false religion which ignores Jesus Christ and has always been an enemy of the Catholic Church.

*Other forbidden societies: Knights of Pythias, Shriners, Odd Fellows, Sons of Temperance, Templars, also the female societies affiliated with them such as the Rebeccas, Eastern Star, Pythian Sisters.*

**11. Why is it a mortal sin to join the Communists?**

Because Communism denies that there is a God and seeks to wipe out religion.

**12. What happens to a Catholic who joins the Masons or Communists?**

A Catholic who knowingly and willingly joins either of these groups commits a mortal sin.

*Traditionally, these offenses were punished by automatic excommunication. Although this penalty no longer applies, joining the Masons or the Communists remains a grave sin.*

**13. Why is it a sin to believe in fortune telling?**

Because to do so is to attribute to a creature knowledge that belongs only to God.

*Only God knows what you will do, and He certainly will not reveal the future in silly ways, such as through tea leaves, the bumps on your head or the lines in your palm.*

**14. Why is it a sin to guide your life by dreams?**

1) God forbids it many times in the Bible.

2) It is foolish and may lead to other sins.

*"Except it be a vision sent forth from the most High, set not thy heart upon them. For dreams have deceived many, and they have failed that put their trust in them." (Ecclesiasticus 34:6-7).*

## PRACTICAL POINTS

1. The Catholic Church is not narrow-minded toward other religions, because it is not being narrow-minded to stay away from error.

**2.** Your attitude toward non-Catholics should be Christian. Try to lead them to the Truth by prayer and good example.

*"Having your conversation good among the Gentiles: that whereas they speak against you as evildoers, they may, by the good work, which they shall behold in you, glorify God in the day of visitation."* (1 Peter 2:12).

# *Lesson 35:*

## The Second Commandment

*"Kings of the earth and all people: princes and all judges of the earth: Young men and maidens: let the old with the younger, praise the name of the Lord: for his name alone is exalted."* (Psalm 148:11-13).

*"But [Our Lord] emptied himself, taking the form of a servant, being made in the likeness of men, and in habit found as a man. He humbled himself, becoming obedient unto death, even to the death of the cross. For which cause God also hath exalted him, and hath given him a name which is above all names: That in the name of Jesus every knee should bow, of those that are in heaven, on earth, and under the earth: And that every tongue should confess that the Lord Jesus Christ is in the glory of God the Father."* (Philippians 2:7-11).

**1. What is the Second Commandment?**

Thou shalt not take the name of the Lord thy God in vain.

*"For the Lord will not hold him guiltless that shall take the name of the Lord his God in vain."* (Exodus 20:7).

**2. What does the Second Commandment oblige you to do?**

Always to use the Name of God and of Jesus Christ reverently.

*"Holy is his name."* (Luke 1:49).

**3. What are the sins against the Second Commandment?**

1) Misusing the Name of God or of Jesus Christ,

2) blasphemy,

3) breaking an oath or lying under oath.

### 4. How may you misuse the name of God?

By using it without good reason and without respect.

*This is generally a venial sin.*

### 5. What is blasphemy?

An expression insulting to God or religion.

*It is a mortal sin when the blasphemer really intends to insult God.*

### 6. What kind of sin is it to use vulgar language?

To say "hell" or "damn" or to use vulgar language usually is no sin at all, unless you mean what you say or say it out of anger or impatience.

*However, these expressions are not fitting for a Christian. "Out of the same mouth proceedeth blessing and cursing. My brethren, these things ought not so to be." (James 3:10).*

### 7. What is an oath?

Calling on God to be witness to the truth.

### 8. What kind of sin is it to lie while under oath?

A mortal sin, called perjury.

*It is mortal, even in a small matter, because an oath calls upon God to witness the lie.*

# *Lesson 36:* The Third Commandment

*"Remember that thou keep holy the sabbath day. Six days shalt thou labour, and shalt do all thy works. But on the seventh day is the sabbath of the Lord thy God: thou shalt do no work on it, thou nor thy son, nor thy daughter, nor thy manservant, nor thy maidservant, nor thy beast, nor the stranger that is within thy gates. For in six days the Lord made heaven and earth, and the sea, and all things that are in them, and rested on the seventh day: therefore the Lord blessed the seventh day, and sanctified it."* (Exodus 20:8-11).

**1. What is the Third Commandment?**

Remember thou keep holy the Sabbath Day.

**2. What does the Third Commandment oblige you to do?**

1) To attend Mass every Sunday and Holy Day of Obligation.

2) To avoid all unnecessary manual ("servile") work or shopping on Sundays and Holy Days.

**3. What are the six Holy Days of Obligation in the United States?**

1) Christmas (Dec. 25), feast of the Birth of Jesus Christ.

2) New Year's Day (Jan. 1), Circumcision of Jesus Christ. (Currently, it is celebrated as the "Solemnity of Mary.")

3) Ascension Thursday (40 days after Easter).

4) Assumption of the Blessed Virgin Mary (Aug. 15).

5) All Saints Day (Nov. 1).

6) Immaculate Conception (Dec. 8).

*In Canada, Epiphany (Jan. 6) is a Holy Day, but the Feast of the Assumption (Aug. 15) is not.*

**4. What kind of sin is it to miss Mass on Sunday or a Holy Day?**

To miss Mass on these days through your own fault and without sufficient reason is a mortal sin.

**5. What kind of sin is it to be late for Mass on a Sunday or Holy Day of Obligation?**

If, through your own fault, you come into the church—

1) anytime before the priest takes the veil off the chalice, you commit a venial sin, unless you stay for the missed part in another Mass;

2) anytime after the priest takes the veil off the chalice, you commit a mortal sin, unless you stay for another entire Mass.

*The priest removing the veil from the chalice marks the beginning of the Offertory, the first of the three principal parts of the Mass.*

**6. Are you ever excused from the obligation of hearing Mass?**

Yes, but only for a serious reason.

*Examples: sickness, caring for a sick person, long distance from the church, necessary work.*

**7. Can a priest excuse you from the obligation?**

Yes, your pastor, or the priest in Confession, can excuse you for a sufficient reason.

*But it is not necessary to ask a priest if you know you have a sufficient reason.*

**8. What does the Third Commandment oblige you to do as a parent?**

You have the serious obligation to see that your children attend Mass on Sundays and Holy Days.

**9. What kind of work is forbidden on Sundays and Holy Days?**

Manual ("servile") work, unless it is necessary, such as making beds, washing dishes, taking care of the sick.

**10. Is it wrong to enjoy sports and other recreation on Sunday?**

No, unless they interfere with your religious obligations.

*Examples: playing games, dancing, movies.*

**11. What kind of sin is it to do unnecessary physical work on Sunday or a Holy Day of Obligation?**

A mortal sin, if you work for a substantial length of time; a venial sin, if for a briefer length of time.

*Unnecessary physical work is considered to be a mortal sin if it totals about 2-1/2 to 3 hours of hard work.*

## NOTE

The Church changed the Lord's Day from Saturday to Sunday because Our Lord rose from the dead on Sunday and the Holy Ghost came down upon the Apostles on Pentecost Sunday. Also, Sunday is the first day of the week and Saturday the last. It is altogether more fitting in the New, more perfect Law or Testament that the Church consecrate the first day of the week to the Lord, rather than the last. Thus we give God the "first fruits" of our week.

# $\mathcal{L}_{ession}$ 37:
## The Fourth Commandment

*"Son, support the old age of thy father, and grieve him not in his life; and if his understanding fail, have patience with him, and despise him not when thou art in thy strength: for the relieving of the father shall not be forgotten. For good shall be repaid to thee for the sin of thy mother. And in justice thou shalt be built up, and in the day of affliction thou shalt be remembered: and thy sins shall melt away as the ice in the fair warm weather."* (Ecclesiasticus 3:14-17).

**1. What is the Fourth Commandment?**

Honor thy father and thy mother.

> *"With thy whole heart, honor thy father, and forget not the groanings of thy mother: Remember that thou hadst not been born but through them: and make a return to them as they have done for thee."* (Ecclesiasticus 7:28-30).

**2. What are the duties of children toward their parents?**

1) To love and respect them as long as they live;

2) to obey them in all things, except sin;

3) to help them in their old age, or when they are sick and helpless;

4) to see that they receive the Last Sacraments and a Catholic funeral; if they are not Catholic, to encourage them to join the True Church.

**3. How long is a child obliged to obey his parents?**

Until approximately the 21st birthday, or until he or she leaves home to be married or to become a priest or sister.

**4. Do your parents come before your marriage partner?**

No, your first obligation is to your marriage partner and your children.

**5. What are the sins against the Fourth Commandment?**

Disobeying one's parents; hating, threatening, cursing, striking or insulting them; being ashamed of them; wishing them evil; speaking or acting unkindly toward them; causing them anger or sorrow.

**6. What else does the Fourth Commandment oblige you to do?**

To respect all lawful authority, especially the authority of the Church and the State.

> *"Let every soul be subject to higher powers: for there is no power but from God: and those that are, are ordained of God. Therefore he that resisteth the power, resisteth the ordinance of God...Render therefore to all men their dues. Tribute, to whom tribute is due: custom, to whom custom: fear, to whom fear: honour, to whom honour."* (Romans 13:1-7).

**7. What are the duties of parents toward their children?**

See Lesson 33, Pages 125-128.

# $\mathcal{L}$εΔΔon 38: The Fifth Commandment

*"And the Lord God formed man of the slime of the earth: and breathed into his face the breath of life, and man became a living soul."* (Genesis 2:7).

**1. What is the Fifth Commandment?**
Thou shalt not kill.

**2. What does the Fifth Commandment oblige you to do?**
To take care of your own life and the lives of others.

**3. What are the mortal sins against the Fifth Commandment?**
1) Murder, the unjust killing of an innocent person.
2) Abortion, deliberately causing the death of an unborn baby.
3) Suicide, taking your own life.
4) "Mercy killing," killing an innocent person who is dying of an incurable disease.
5) Causing serious injury or death by criminal neglect.
6) Sterilization, making the sex organs unfruitful.
7) Getting drunk.
8) Serious anger and hatred.
9) Helping another to commit a mortal sin.

**4. Are you ever allowed to use force or to kill?**
Only in self-defense, when it is the only way you can protect yourself or another and when you or someone else is being seriously attacked here and now.

> You may kill in defense of life, bodily integrity, chastity or material goods of great value. If possible, you should flee from the attacker, or wound him rather than kill him.

**5. Is abortion ever allowed?**

No, because deliberately to take the life of any innocent person, even that of an unborn baby, is murder.

*Any Catholic who knowingly and willingly has an abortion is automatically excommunicated from the Church, and anyone who helps someone to procure an abortion commits a mortal sin. See Page 115, Lesson 30, Questions 13 and 14.*

**6. Is suicide ever allowed?**

No, your life belongs to God, and He alone can take it away.

*A Catholic who commits suicide while in his right mind loses his right to have a Catholic funeral.*

**7. Is "mercy killing" ever allowed?**

No, because it is murder.

*A person who allows himself to be killed in this way is guilty of suicide.*

**8. Is sterilization ever allowed?**

To have the Fallopian tubes or the seminal vesicles (sperm ducts) tied or cut is always a mortal sin.

*The reproductive organs may be removed only when they are diseased and present a danger to the whole body.*

**9. What kind of sin is it to get drunk?**

To get slightly drunk is a venial sin; to get seriously drunk is a mortal sin.

*You are guilty of any sins you commit while under the influence of alcohol, even though later on you do not remember committing them.*

**10. Are you ever allowed to use narcotics?**

Only when recommended by a competent doctor, and then only according to his directions.

**11. Are hatred and anger mortal sins?**

Hatred of another person is a mortal sin and anger toward another person is usually a venial sin, unless you wish someone serious harm.

## 12. Is there such a thing as sinless anger?

Yes, anger prompted by zeal for justice, honor to God, or some other good cause.

*Jesus, for example, was angry with the buyers and sellers in the temple.*

## 13. In what other way can you sin against the Fifth Commandment?

By helping another to commit sin by your sinful actions or words, or by giving another whatever is necessary to commit sin.

*"But he that shall scandalize one of these little ones that believe in me, it were better for him that a millstone should be hanged about his neck, and that he should be drowned in the depth of the sea." (Matthew 18:6).*

## 14. Is capital punishment (the death penalty) ever allowed?

Yes, the state has the right to administer the death penalty for a grave crime in the interest of the common welfare.

## 15. Can there ever be a just war?

Yes, both offensive and defensive wars are lawful for a serious and just cause if there is no other means to obtain justice.

# Lesson 39:
## The Sixth and Ninth Commandments

*"But the body is not for fornication, but for the Lord, and the Lord for the body. Now God hath both raised up the Lord, and will raise us up also by his power. Know you not that your bodies are the members of Christ? Shall I then take the members of Christ, and make them the members of an harlot? God forbid. Or know you not, that he who is joined to a harlot, is made one body? For they shall be, saith he, two in one flesh. But he who is joined to the Lord, is one spirit. Fly fornication. Every sin that a man doth, is without the body; but he that committeth fornication, sinneth against his own body. Or know you not, that your members are the temple of the Holy Ghost, who is in you, whom you have from God; and you are not your own? For you are bought with a great price. Glorify and bear God in your body."* (1 Corinthians 6:13-20).

**1. What is the Sixth Commandment?**
Thou shalt not commit adultery.

**2. What is the Ninth Commandment?**
Thou shalt not covet thy neighbor's wife.

**3. What do these commandments oblige you to do?**
To practice the virtue of chastity according to your state in life.

> Chastity regulates the use of sex for married people. Chastity forbids any use of sex, complete or incomplete, to unmarried people. This also includes those who are engaged.

**4. Who are the only ones who may engage in sex?**
Only husband and wife who are validly married to each other, and only in the natural manner, with their proper marriage partner, and only in a manner that leaves open the conception of a child.

**5. Name some of the sins against the Sixth Commandment.**

Adultery          Birth Control
Fornication       Sins against nature
Self-abuse        Immodest dressing
Impure touches, looks, kisses, dancing, reading.
Looking at impure pictures, dances, shows, movies.
Keeping company with people who are a temptation.

**6. What is adultery?**

Sexual intercourse which a married person has with someone to whom he (or she) is not married.

*"For fornicators and adulterers God will judge."* (Hebrews 13:4).
*"Neither fornicators...nor adulterers...shall possess the kingdom of God."* (1 Corinthians 6:9-10).

**7. What is fornication?**

Sexual intercourse between an unmarried man and an unmarried woman.

**8. What is self-abuse?**

Enjoying the sexual pleasure alone; also called masturbation.

**9. What are sins against nature?**

Perversions committed with oneself, with another person or with animals.

*"Do not err: neither fornicators, nor idolaters, nor adulterers, nor the effeminate, nor liers with mankind [i.e., practicing homosexuals] shall possess the kingdom of God."* (1 Corinthians 6:9-10).

**10. What is forbidden by the Ninth Commandment?**

Impure thoughts and desires.

*"But I say to you that whosoever shall look on a woman to lust after her, hath already committed adultery with her in his heart."* (Matthew 5:28).

## 11. What kind of sin are sins of sex—that is, all impure acts, thoughts and desires?

Every sin of impurity is a mortal sin, unless not fully consented to, as could happen, for example, with impure thoughts.

*A temptation is not a sin. If you reject a temptation, you do a good act and receive extra grace.*

## 12. When do you become guilty of impure thoughts?

When you knowingly and willingly keep such thoughts in your mind, but especially in taking pleasure in them.

*"For from within out of the heart of men proceed evil thoughts, adulteries, fornications, murders."* (Mark 7:21).

## 13. Is it possible to lead a pure life?

Yes, with God's help—

1) if you stay away from all persons, places or things which easily lead into sin;

2) if you pray often (especially to the Blessed Virgin Mary and especially pray her holy Rosary) and go to Confession and receive Communion regularly;

3) if you keep busy;

4) if you *flee* from temptations when they first appear (do not "toy" with sexual temptations);

5) if you practice giving up things you like and doing things you do not like.

*"And every one that striveth for the mastery, refraineth himself from all things: and they indeed that they may receive a corruptible crown; but we an incorruptible one."* (1 Corinthians 9:25).

## PRACTICAL POINTS

1. A Catholic today must bear in mind that he is living in a mostly pagan world and that many things which the world takes for granted are in fact sins or at least serious temptations that must be avoided. Television shows, videos, wearing apparel, etc. must be evaluated with a Catholic conscience and not with the eyes of the world.

# $\mathcal{L}$ɛsson 40:

## The Seventh and Tenth Commandments

*"Thou shalt not steal."* (Exodus 20:15). *"A thief is better than a man that is always lying: but both of them shall inherit destruction."* (Ecclesiasticus 20:27). *"He that stealeth any thing from his father, or from his mother: and saith, This is no sin, is the partner of a murderer."* (Proverbs 28:24). *"Nor thieves, nor covetous...nor extortioners, shall possess the kingdom of God."* (Corinthians 6:9-10). *"He that stole, let him now steal no more; but rather let him labor, working with his hands the thing which is good, that he may have something to give to him that suffereth need."* (Ephesians 4:28). *"Envies, murders, drunkenness, revellings, and such like. Of the which I foretell you, as I have foretold to you, that they who do such things shall not obtain the kingdom of God."* (Galatians 5:21).

**1. What is the Seventh Commandment?**
Thou shalt not steal.

**2. What does the Seventh Commandment oblige you to do?**
To respect the property of others.

**3. What is meant by stealing?**
Taking anything which does not belong to you and which the owner is not willing to give you.

**4. What sins does stealing include?**
Robbery and burglary.
Graft, bribes and embezzlement.
Cheating and fraud.
Not paying bills, taxes and debts.
Not supporting your family.

Damaging the property of others.

Wasting time or materials on your job.

Not giving employees a just wage.

## 5. What kind of sin is it to steal?

Stealing something expensive is a mortal sin; stealing something cheap is a venial sin.

## 6. Are you ever allowed to keep stolen goods?

No, you have to give the goods back to the person from whom they were stolen, whether you stole them yourself or got them from somebody else.

*No matter how small the theft—silverware, ash trays, towels—you must give it back.*

## 7. What must you do if you cannot find the owner?

Give the stolen goods to charity, or give a comparable amount of money.

## 8. What must you do if you damage someone's property?

You must pay for the damage, or else be guilty of sin.

*The sin is mortal or venial depending on the value of the object damaged or destroyed.*

## 9. What should you do with something you find?

Try to find the owner.

*If the article is expensive, then you must spend some money advertising for him. He has to pay you the money you spent in trying to find him.*

## 10. Is gambling a sin?

It is no sin to gamble if—

1) it is your money, and

2) you do not thereby deprive your family of the things they need, and

3) everyone has an equal chance to win.

**11. What are the duties of employees?**

1) Not to waste time or materials.

2) To do the job assigned as well as possible.

**12. What are the duties of employers?**

1) To pay their employees a just wage.

2) To provide for the safety of all employees.

**13. What is the Tenth Commandment?**

Thou shalt not covet thy neighbor's goods.

**14. How do you sin against the Tenth Commandment?**

By desiring to steal someone else's property and by envy or jealousy, that is, resentment over someone else's good fortune or wishing he did not have it.

*You can be jealous and envious of someone's beauty, intelligence, holiness, etc., as well as of his or her material goods. Jealousy is also called discontent.*

**15. What kind of sins are jealousy and envy?**

Usually venial sins, unless they involve a serious matter; then they are mortal.

*Remember that temptation is not a sin, unless you accept the envious feelings. If you reject them, you do a good act and receive more Sanctifying Grace from God in return.*

# $\mathcal{L}$esson 41:
## The Eighth Commandment

*"And the tongue is a fire, a world of iniquity. The tongue is placed among our members, which defileth the whole body, and inflameth the wheel of our nativity, being set on fire by hell. For every nature of beasts, and of birds, and of serpents, and of the rest, is tamed, and hath been tamed, by the nature of man: But the tongue no man can tame, an unquiet evil, full of deadly poison. By it we bless God and the Father: and by it we curse men, who are made after the likeness of God. Out of the same mouth proceedeth blessing and cursing. My brethren, these things ought not so to be."* (James 3:6-10).

### 1. What is the Eighth Commandment?
Thou shalt not bear false witness against thy neighbor.

### 2. What does the Eighth Commandment oblige you to do?
To use the power of speech according to God's plan, that is, always to tell the truth.

### 3. Name some of the sins against the Eighth Commandment.

Lying

Hurting someone's reputation

Unjust criticism

Gossip

Insults

Perjury

Not keeping secrets

Making known the sins of others

Judging another without sufficient evidence (rash judgment)

Suspecting another without sufficient evidence (rash suspicion)

**4. What kind of sin is it to tell a lie?**

A mortal sin, if it harms someone seriously; otherwise, it is venial.

**5. Are you ever allowed to tell a lie?**

No, not even a small one, not even to save someone's life or reputation.

*"Wherefore putting away lying, speak ye the truth every man with his neighbour; for we are members one of another."* (Ephesians 4:25).

**6. What must you do if you have told lies about another?**

You have to do everything you can to restore his good name and make up any losses he suffered because of your lies.

**7. Is it a sin to make known the hidden sins of another?**

Yes, unless someone else would suffer harm; in such a case you are obliged to tell the proper authorities.

**8. Is it a sin to listen to gossip?**

Yes, because you are co-operating in another's sin.

*It is a duty of charity to defend the reputation of another when it is being attacked.*

**9. Is perjury a sin?**

Telling a lie after swearing to God to tell the truth is always a mortal sin.

*"A false witness shall not be unpunished: and he that speaketh lies, shall perish."* (Proverbs 19:9).

# Lesson 42:  Charity

*"And one of them, a doctor of the law, asked him, tempting him: Master, which is the great commandment in the law? Jesus said to him:* Thou shalt love the Lord thy God with thy whole heart, and with thy whole soul, and with thy whole mind. *This is the greatest and the first commandment. And the second is like to this:* Thou shalt love thy neighbour as thyself. *On these two commandments dependeth the whole law and the prophets."* (Matthew 22:35-40).

### 1. What is charity?

Tho virtue by which you love God above all things and your neighbor as yourself for the love of God.

*"And now there remain faith, hope and charity, these three: but the greatest of these is charity."* (1 Corinthians 13:13).

### 2. What is the love of God?

Perfect love is love of God because He is supremely perfect and good in Himself; whereas, imperfect love is based on gratitude for benefits received and hope for benefits to come.

### 3. Can you love God without loving your neighbor?

No, because "If any man say, I love God, and hateth his brother; he is a liar. For he that loveth not his brother, whom he seeth, how can he love God, whom he seeth not?" (1 John 4:20).

### 4. Who is your neighbor?

Every human being on earth, the souls in Purgatory, the Angels and Saints.

**153**

## 5. How should you love your neighbor?

1) Wishing him well for the love of God.

2) Performing the spiritual and corporal works of mercy.

## 6. What are the spiritual works of mercy?

1) To admonish the sinner.

2) To instruct the ignorant.

3) To counsel the doubtful.

4) To comfort the sorrowful.

5) To bear wrongs patiently.

6) To forgive all injuries.

7) To pray for the living and the dead.

## 7. What are the corporal works of mercy?

1) To feed the hungry.

2) To give drink to the thirsty.

3) To clothe the naked.

4) To ransom the captive.

5) To shelter the homeless.

6) To visit the sick.

7) To bury the dead.

> *"To ransom the captive"* was put in this list obviously from the days when Moslems took Christians captive as slaves. Perhaps this currently less common work of mercy should be replaced by *"To save the pre-born,"* now that abortion is so prevalent.

## 8. What are some sins against charity?

Thinking or speaking unkindly of others.

Acting unkindly toward others.

Hatred.

Envy.

Causing discord.

Scandal.

Co-operating in the sins of others.

Not forgiving those who have offended you.

Not helping those who need your help.

# ℒℯ𝓈𝓈ℴ𝓃 43: Fast and Abstinence

*"And Jesus being full of the Holy Ghost, returned from the Jordan, and was led by the Spirit into the desert, for the space of forty days; and was tempted by the devil. And he ate nothing in those days; and when they were ended, he was hungry."* (Luke 4:1-2).

## 1. What is fasting?

Fasting means that on certain days, you may eat—

1) one full meal with meat (unless it is also a day of abstinence);

2) two small meals without meat,

3) no food between meals.

> *A fast day consists of 24 hours, from midnight to midnight. The two small meals may be only enough to maintain strength and are not to exceed the size of the one main meal. Liquids, including milk and fruit juice, may be taken between meals, but tend to violate the spirit of the fast.*

## 2. Who is obliged to fast?

Every Catholic over 21 and not yet 59, who is not sick, pregnant or nursing a baby.

> *People doing heavy manual labor may be excused from this obligation by their pastor or confessor; also, those who work long hours.*

## 3. What kind of sin is it not to fast?

A mortal sin, unless you are excused.

## 4. When must you fast?

According to the old norms:

1) Every day in Lent, except Sundays.

2) December 7, December 24 (or 23) and the Saturday before Pentecost.

3) Ember Days.

*Some Catholics continue this tradition. According to the new norms, there are only 2 fast days: Ash Wednesday and Good Friday.*

## 5. When does Lent begin?

On Ash Wednesday; it ends 40 days later, on the Saturday before Easter at midnight.

## 6. When are the Ember Days?

The Wednesdays, Fridays and Saturdays following September 14, December 13, Pentecost Sunday and the 1st Sunday in Lent.

*Under the new norms the Ember Days are no longer observed.*

## 7. What is abstinence?

Abstinence means that on certain days you may not eat meat.

## 8. What is meant by "meat"?

The flesh of any warm-blooded animal or bird and the soups or gravies made from such flesh.

*Seafoods are allowed (fish, lobster, turtles, crabs, oysters, frogs, scallops, clams, and so on).*

## 9. Who is obliged to abstain from meat?

Traditionally, every Catholic 7 years of age and over.

*According to the new norms, every Catholic 14 years of age and over is obliged to abstain.*

## 10. What kind of sin is it not to abstain?

A mortal sin.

**11. On what days are you forbidden to eat meat at all?**

According to the old norms: Ash Wednesday, all Fridays of the year (unless a Holy Day of Obligation falls on Friday), December 7 and December 24 (or 23). Some Catholics continue this tradition. According to the new norms: 1) Ash Wednesday and 2) Every Friday of Lent.

*According to the new norms, on every Friday of the year outside Lent Catholics must either abstain from meat or do some other comparable penance, unless the Friday falls on a Holy Day of Obligation, in which case one is excused from abstinence.*

**12. What is partial abstinence?**

Traditionally, this means that those who are obliged to abstain may eat meat only once (at the main meal) on the Wednesdays and Saturdays of Ember weeks and on the vigil of Pentecost.

*Under the new norms there are no longer any days of partial abstinence.*

# Prayers

## 1. The Sign of the Cross

In the name of the Father, and of the Son, and of the Holy Ghost. Amen.

## 2. The Our Father

Our Father, Who art in Heaven, hallowed be Thy name. Thy kingdom come, Thy will be done, on earth as it is in Heaven. Give us this day our daily bread, and forgive us our trespasses as we forgive those who trespass against us, and lead us not into temptation, but deliver us from evil. Amen.

## 3. The Hail Mary

Hail Mary, full of grace, the Lord is with thee. Blessed art thou among women and blessed is the fruit of thy womb, Jesus. Holy Mary, Mother of God, pray for us sinners now and at the hour of our death. Amen.

## 4. The Apostles' Creed

I believe in God, the Father Almighty, Creator of Heaven and earth, and in Jesus Christ His only Son Our Lord, who was conceived by the Holy Ghost, born of the Virgin Mary, suffered under Pontius Pilate, was crucified, died and was buried. He descended into hell; the third day He arose again from the dead; He ascended into Heaven, sitteth at the right hand of God, the Father Almighty; from thence He shall come to judge the living and the dead. I believe in the Holy Ghost, the Holy Catholic Church, the Communion of Saints, the forgiveness of sins, the resurrection of the body, and life everlasting. Amen.

## 5. Glory be to the Father

Glory be to the Father, and to the Son, and to the Holy Ghost, as it was in the beginning, is now and ever shall be, world without end. Amen.

## 6. Act of Contrition

O my God, I am heartily sorry for having offended Thee, and I detest all my sins, because I dread the loss of Heaven and the pains of Hell, but most of all, because they offend Thee, my God, Who art all good and deserving of all my love. I firmly resolve, with the help of Thy grace, to confess my sins, to do penance and to amend my life. Amen.

## 7. Blessing before eating

Bless us, O Lord, and these Thy gifts, which we are about to receive from Thy bounty, through Christ Our Lord. Amen.

## 8. Thanks after eating

We give Thee thanks, Almighty God, for these and all Thy gifts which we have received from Thy bounty through Christ Our Lord. Amen. May the souls of the faithful departed through the mercy of God, rest in peace. Amen.

## 9. Act of Faith

O my God, I firmly believe that Thou art one God in three Divine Persons, Father, Son and Holy Ghost. I believe that Thy Divine Son became man and died for our sins, and that He will come to judge the living and the dead. I believe these and all the truths which the Holy Catholic Church teaches, because Thou hast revealed them, Who canst neither deceive nor be deceived.

## 10. Act of Hope

O my God, relying on Thy almighty power and infinite mercy and promises, I hope to obtain pardon of my sins, the help of Thy grace, and life everlasting, through the merits of Jesus Christ, my Lord and Redeemer. Amen.

## 11. Act of Love

O my God, I love Thee above all things, with my whole heart and soul, because Thou art all good and worthy of all my love. I love my neighbor as myself for the love of Thee. I forgive all who have injured me and ask pardon of all whom I have injured. Amen.

## 12. Hail, Holy Queen

Hail, Holy Queen, Mother of Mercy, our life, our sweetness and our hope! To thee do we cry, poor banished children of Eve; to thee do we send up our sighs, mourning and weeping in this valley of tears! Turn then, most gracious Advocate, thine eyes of mercy towards us, and after this our exile, show unto us the blessed Fruit of thy womb, Jesus. O clement, O loving, O sweet Virgin Mary.
*V.* Pray for us, O holy Mother of God,
*R.* That we may be made worthy of the promises of Christ.

## 13. The Confiteor

I confess to Almighty God, to blessed Mary ever Virgin, to blessed Michael the Archangel, to blessed John the Baptist, to the holy Apostles Peter and Paul, and to all the Saints that I have sinned exceedingly in thought, word and deed, through my fault, through my fault, through my most grievous fault. Therefore, I beseech blessed Mary ever Virgin, blessed Michael the Archangel, blessed John the Baptist, the holy Apostles Peter and Paul, and all the Saints to pray to the Lord our God for me.

May Almighty God have mercy on me, forgive me my sins and bring me to life everlasting. Amen.

May the Almighty and merciful Lord grant me pardon, absolution and remission of all my sins. Amen.

## 14. The Memorare

Remember, O most gracious Virgin Mary, that never was it known that anyone who ever fled to thy protection, implored thy help or sought thy intercession was left unaided. Inspired by this confidence, I fly unto thee, O Virgin of virgins, my Mother. To thee do I come, before thee I kneel, sinful and sorrowful. O Mother of the Word Incarnate, despise not my petitions, but in thy mercy hear and answer them. Amen.

## 15. Morning Prayers

In the name of the Father, and of the Son, and of the Holy Ghost. Amen.

O Jesus, through the Immaculate Heart of Mary, I offer Thee all my prayers, works, joys and sufferings of this day, for all the intentions of Thy Sacred Heart, in union with the Holy Sacrifice of the Mass throughout the world, in reparation for all my sins, for the intentions of all our associates, but in particular for the special intentions of the Blessed Virgin Mary. I wish to gain all the indulgences attached to the prayers I shall say and the good works I shall do this day. Help me to avoid sin today.

Our Father, Who art in Heaven...
Hail Mary...
I believe in God...
Glory be to the Father...
Acts of Faith, Hope and Love. (Pages 158-160).

Angel of God, my guardian dear, to whom His love commits me here, ever this day be at my side, to light and guard, to rule and guide. Amen.

O Mary, my Queen and my Mother, I give myself entirely to thee. And to show my devotion to thee, I consecrate to thee this day, my eyes, my ears, my mouth, my heart, and my whole being, without reserve. Wherefore, since I am thine, O loving Mother, keep me and guard me as thy property and possession. Amen.

In the name of the Father, and of the Son, and of the Holy Ghost. Amen.

## 16. Evening Prayers

In the name of the Father, and of the Son, and of the Holy Ghost. Amen.

Our Father...Hail Mary...I believe in God...Glory be...

O my God, I thank Thee for Thy benefits, especially those which I have received today from Thy bounty. Give me the light to know what sins I have committed today and the grace to be sorry for them.

*(Now examine in your mind the day's activities and find out what sins you have committed today.)*

### Act of Contrition

O my God, I am heartily sorry for having offended Thee, and I detest all my sins because I dread the loss of Heaven and the pains of Hell, but most of all because they offend Thee, my God, Who art all good and deserving of all my love. I firmly resolve, with the help of Thy grace, to confess my sins, to do penance and to amend my life. Amen.

Jesus, Mary and Joseph, I give thee my heart and my soul.
Jesus, Mary and Joseph, assist me in my last agony.
Jesus, Mary and Joseph, may I breathe forth my soul in peace with thee. Amen.

May the Lord bless me and bring me to life everlasting, and may the souls of the faithful departed, through the mercy of God, rest in peace. Amen.

In the name of the Father, and of the Son, and of the Holy Ghost. Amen.

## 17. Prayers for going to Confession

O loving and merciful God, help me to make a good Confession. Help me to know my sins, so that I may be able to tell the priest what sins I have committed and how often I have committed them. Grant me a deep sorrow for all my sins, and grant me the help necessary not to sin again.

*(Now look into your memory and see what sins you have committed since your last Confession and how many times you committed each sin, as closely as you can recall.)*

## A List of Some Mortal Sins

1) Missing Mass on Sunday or on a Holy Day.

2) Coming late to Mass on a Sunday or Holy Day—after the priest has removed the veil from the chalice.

3) Not making your Easter duty.

4) Receiving Holy Communion in the state of mortal sin.

5) Doing unnecessary physical work on Sunday or on a Holy Day of Obligation (about 2-1/2 to 3 hours or more).

6) Eating meat on a forbidden day, when you know it is a forbidden day; or not fasting on a fast day.

7) Getting drunk.

8) Adultery.

9) Fornication.

10) Self-abuse (masturbation).

11) Impure touches or kisses.

12) Impure looks or thoughts or desires.

13) Impure dancing.

14) Impure talk.

15) Watching sexually immoral movies or videos.

16) Reading sexually immoral books or literature.

17) Looking at immodest or immoral pictures.

18) Unnatural sins of sex.

19) Birth control.

20) Refusing intercourse to your husband (or wife) without serious reason.

21) "Marriage" outside the Catholic Church.

22) Receiving Holy Communion while living in a "marriage" outside the Catholic Church.
23) Keeping company with someone who is still married in the eyes of God (a divorced or separated person).
24) Gambling away the family money.
25) Stealing something expensive, or a large sum of money (more than the daily wage of the person you steal from).
26) Giving bad example to your children in serious matters.
27) Murder or seriously harming another.
28) Killing an unborn baby (abortion).
29) Sterilization.
30) Serious anger.
31) Hatred.
32) Driving while seriously intoxicated.
33) Helping another commit a mortal sin.
34) Telling serious lies about another.
35) Revealing serious wrongdoing by someone without good reason.
36) Telling a lie after swearing to tell the truth.
37) Not supporting your family.
38) Seriously neglecting your children.
39) Wishing someone serious harm.
40) Breaking a serious contract.
41) Cursing someone.
42) Guiding your life by horoscopes, fortune telling or superstition.
43) Using a ouija board.
44) Trying to contact spirits.
45) Insulting God or His holy religion.
46) Reading non-Catholic Bibles or books about religion.
47) Denying anything taught by the Catholic Church.
48) Taking part in false (non-Catholic) religious services.

## A List of Some Venial Sins

1) Ordinary anger.
2) Impatience.
3) Lies which harm no one.
4) Gossip.
5) Not obeying in ordinary matters.
6) Criticizing others.
7) Getting slightly drunk.
8) Speaking or thinking unkindly of others.
9) Eating too much.
10) Stealing something inexpensive, or a small amount of money.

### Act of Contrition

O my God, I am heartily sorry for having offended Thee, and I detest all my sins because I dread the loss of Heaven and the pains of Hell, but most of all because they offend Thee, my God, Who art all good and deserving of all my love. I firmly resolve, with the help of Thy grace, to confess my sins, to do penance and to amend my life. Amen.

## 18. Prayer after Confession

O Almighty and Merciful God, I thank Thee for all the blessings which Thou hast given me, but especially for forgiving my sins. Give me the strength necessary to overcome my temptations and to be always faithful to Thee. I wish to renew the promises I made when I was baptized, and from this moment I give myself entirely to Thy love and service. Let nothing in life or death separate me from Thee. Through Jesus Christ Our Lord. Amen.

## 19. Prayers for the dead

Eternal rest grant unto him (her, them), O Lord, and let perpetual light shine upon him (her, them). May his (her, their) soul(s) and the souls of all the faithful departed, through the mercy of God, rest in peace. Amen.

## 20. Prayers after receiving Holy Communion

O Jesus, I firmly believe that Thou art really and truly present in the Blessed Sacrament. Although my eyes and tongue tell me that I have received only bread, yet my faith tells me that I have received Thy Body and Blood. I believe, Lord; help Thou my unbelief. I adore Thee as my God and my Saviour.

O Jesus, I love Thee above all things. Never let anything separate me from Thy love. Inflame my cold heart with the fire of Thy love.

My loving Jesus, I wish to offer Thee my sincere thanks for coming to me in Holy Communion. How can I repay Thee for all that Thou hast done for me? Everything I shall ever do and say shall be for Thee.

O Jesus dwelling within me, please forgive me for my sins. By them I have caused Thee great sorrow. Never permit me to sin again, but let me always love Thee. Strengthen me and bless me by the power of this Holy Sacrament, now and at the hour of my death. Amen.

## 21. Prayers for the Conversion of Russia traditionally said at the end of Low Mass

Hail Mary (three times).

Priest: Hail, Holy Queen,
People: Mother of Mercy, our life, our sweetness and our hope! To thee do we cry, poor banished children of Eve; to thee do we send up our sighs, mourning and weeping in this valley of tears! Turn, then, most gracious Advocate, thine eyes of mercy towards us, and after

this our exile, show unto us the blessed Fruit of thy womb, Jesus. O clement, O loving, O sweet Virgin Mary!

Priest: Pray for us, O holy Mother of God,

People: That we may be made worthy of the promises of Christ.

Priest: Let us pray.

People: O God, our refuge and our strength, look down with favor upon Thy people who cry to Thee, and through the intercession of the glorious and immaculate Virgin Mary, Mother of God, of Saint Joseph her spouse, of Thy holy Apostles Peter and Paul and of all the Saints, mercifully and graciously hear the prayers which we pour forth to Thee for the conversion of sinners and for the freedom and exaltation of Holy Mother the Church. Through the same Christ Our Lord.

People: Amen.

All: St. Michael, the Archangel, defend us in battle. Be our protection against the wickedness and snares of the devil. May God rebuke him, we humbly pray. And do thou, O Prince of the heavenly host, by the power of God, cast into Hell Satan and the other evil spirits who wander about the world seeking the ruin and destruction of souls. Amen.

Priest: Most Sacred Heart of Jesus,

People: Have mercy on us!

Priest: Most Sacred Heart of Jesus,

People: Have mercy on us!

Priest: Most Sacred Heart of Jesus,

People: Have mercy on us!

# How To Say The Rosary

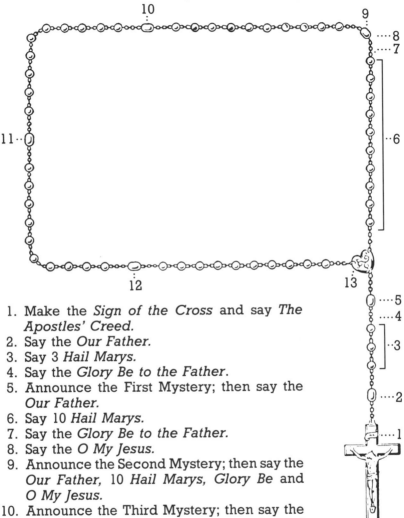

1. Make the *Sign of the Cross* and say *The Apostles' Creed.*
2. Say the *Our Father.*
3. Say 3 *Hail Marys.*
4. Say the *Glory Be to the Father.*
5. Announce the First Mystery; then say the *Our Father.*
6. Say 10 *Hail Marys.*
7. Say the *Glory Be to the Father.*
8. Say the *O My Jesus.*
9. Announce the Second Mystery; then say the *Our Father,* 10 *Hail Marys, Glory Be* and *O My Jesus.*
10. Announce the Third Mystery; then say the *Our Father,* 10 *Hail Marys, Glory Be* and *O My Jesus.*
11. Announce the Fourth Mystery; then say the *Our Father,* 10 *Hail Marys, Glory Be* and *O My Jesus.*
12. Announce the Fifth Mystery; then say the *Our Father,* 10 *Hail Marys, Glory Be* and *O My Jesus.*
13. Conclude by saying the *Hail, Holy Queen.*

# Prayers of the Rosary

## The Apostles' Creed

I believe in God, the Father Almighty, Creator of heaven and earth, and in Jesus Christ, His only Son, our Lord, who was conceived by the Holy Ghost, born of the Virgin Mary, suffered under Pontius Pilate, was crucified, died, and was buried. He descended into Hell; the third day He arose again from the dead; He ascended into Heaven, sitteth at the right hand of God, the Father Almighty; from thence He shall come to judge the living and the dead. *I believe in the Holy Ghost, the holy Catholic Church, the Communion of Saints, the forgiveness of sins, the resurrection of the body, and life everlasting. Amen.

## The Our Father

Our Father, Who art in Heaven, hallowed be Thy name. Thy kingdom come, Thy will be done on earth as it is in Heaven. *Give us this day our daily bread and forgive us our trespasses, as we forgive those who trespass against us, and lead us not into temptation, but deliver us from evil. Amen.

## The Hail Mary

Hail Mary, full of grace, the Lord is with thee; blessed art thou among women, and blessed is the Fruit of thy womb, Jesus. *Holy Mary, Mother of God, pray for us sinners, now and at the hour of our death. Amen.

## The Glory Be

Glory be to the Father, and to the Son, and to the Holy Ghost; *as it was in the beginning, is now and ever shall be, world without end. Amen.

## O My Jesus

O my Jesus, forgive us our sins, save us from the fires of Hell, lead all souls to Heaven, especially those in most need of Thy mercy.

---

*When the Rosary is prayed aloud in a group, the leader recites the first part of these prayers; then the rest of the congregation picks up and recites the latter part beginning at the asterisk.*

## The Hail Holy Queen

Hail, Holy Queen, Mother of Mercy, our life, our sweetness and our hope! To thee do we cry, poor banished children of Eve; to thee do we send up our sighs, mourning and weeping in this valley of tears! Turn then, most gracious Advocate, thine eyes of mercy towards us, and after this our exile, show unto us the blessed Fruit of thy womb, Jesus. O clement, O loving, O sweet Virgin Mary!

V. Pray for us, O holy Mother of God,

R. That we may be made worthy of the promises of Christ.

Let us pray.

O God, Whose only-begotten Son, by His life, death and Resurrection, hast purchased for us the rewards of eternal salvation, grant, we beseech Thee, that meditating upon these mysteries of the most holy Rosary of the Blessed Virgin Mary, we may both imitate what they contain and obtain what they promise, through the same Christ Our Lord. Amen.

# The Mysteries of the Rosary

The Rosary is a series of familiar prayers during which you think on events in the life of Jesus and of His Blessed Mother. These events are called *"Mysteries."* The Mysteries are divided into three groups:

## THE JOYFUL MYSTERIES

*Usually prayed on Mondays and Thursdays and on Sundays from Advent until Lent.*

1. THE ANNUNCIATION. The Angel Gabriel announces to Mary that God wants her to be His Mother.
2. THE VISITATION. Mary visits her cousin Elizabeth.
3. THE NATIVITY. Jesus is born in Bethlehem.
4. THE PRESENTATION. Jesus is presented in the Temple.
5. THE FINDING IN THE TEMPLE. Jesus is found in the Temple.

## THE SORROWFUL MYSTERIES

*Usually prayed on Tuesdays and Fridays and on the Sundays in Lent.*

1. THE AGONY IN THE GARDEN. Jesus sweats blood.
2. THE SCOURGING AT THE PILLAR. Jesus is cruelly scourged.
3. THE CROWNING WITH THORNS. Jesus is crowned.
4. THE CARRYING OF THE CROSS. Jesus carries His Cross.
5. THE CRUCIFIXION. Jesus dies on the Cross.

## THE GLORIOUS MYSTERIES

*Usually prayed on Wednesdays and Saturdays and on Sunday from Easter until Advent.*

1. THE RESURRECTION. Jesus rises from the dead.
2. THE ASCENSION. Jesus ascends into Heaven.
3. THE DESCENT OF THE HOLY GHOST upon the Apostles.
4. THE ASSUMPTION. The Blessed Virgin Mary is taken up to Heaven, body and soul.
5. THE CORONATION. Mary is crowned Queen of Heaven and earth.

# The Stations of the Cross

The Stations of the Cross is a devotion which consists in following Our Lord in spirit on His sorrowful journey from Pilate's palace to His death and burial on Mount Calvary. In the early days of the Church, Christians used to trace the steps Our Lord took in carrying His Cross, but since most people could not make the trip to Jerusalem, the Church instituted the devotion known as the Stations of the Cross. In every Catholic church, you will see fourteen pictures or carvings which help you to recall the principal events of Christ's last hours. "Making the Stations" means that you walk from the first Station to the fourteenth, pausing at each one to meditate on the scene represented and to offer some prayers. Here are the titles of the Stations of the Cross:

1st. Jesus is condemned to death.

2nd. Jesus carries His Cross.

3rd. Jesus falls the first time.

4th. Jesus meets His afflicted Mother.

5th. Simon of Cyrene helps Jesus to carry His Cross.

6th. Veronica wipes the face of Jesus.

7th. Jesus falls the second time.

8th. The Daughters of Jerusalem weep over Jesus.

9th. Jesus falls the third time.

10th. Jesus is stripped of His garments.

11th. Jesus is nailed to the Cross.

12th. Jesus dies on the Cross.

13th. Jesus is taken down from the Cross.

14th. Jesus is buried in the tomb.

# INSIDE PLAN OF A CATHOLIC CHURCH

**ALTAR BOYS' SACRISTY**
(Where the boys who help the Priest at Mass vest)

*Sanctuary Light

**Tabernacle**

**Main Altar**

**PRIESTS' SACRISTY**
(Where the Priest puts on special vestments for Mass)

*Side Altar*

Pulpit

*Side Altar*

# S A N C T U A R Y

*Communion Rail*

*Gospel Side of Church*

*Epistle Side of Church*

1st

14th

2nd

13th

**Center Aisle**

**━ PEWS ━**
⌐ *Where the People Sit* ¬

**━ PEWS ━**
⌐ *Where the People Sit* ¬

3rd

Stations of the Cross

12th

Stations of the Cross

4th

11th

5th

10th

6th

9th

7th

8th

*Confessional*

| You kneel in here for Confession | Priest sits here | You kneel in here for Confession |

/ Holy Water Fonts \

*Confessional*

| You kneel in here for Confession | Priest sits here | You kneel in here for Confession |

Front Doors of Church

**173**

# Some Saints' Names for Baptism and Confirmation

## MEN

| | | | |
|---|---|---|---|
| Albert | Francis | Lawrence | Paul |
| Andrew | George | Leonard | Peter |
| Anthony | Gerard | Louis | Philip |
| Augustine | Gregory | Luke | Raymond |
| Benedict | Henry | Marcel | Richard |
| Bernard | Hugh | Mark | Robert |
| Charles | Ignatius | Martin | Sebastian |
| Christopher | James | Matthew | Stephen |
| Damian | Jerome | Matthias | Thomas |
| Daniel | John | Michael | Timothy |
| David | Joseph | Nathaniel | Vincent |
| Dominic | Jude | Nicholas | William |
| Edward | Justin | Patrick | Xavier |

## WOMEN

| | | | |
|---|---|---|---|
| Agnes | Dorothy | Josephine | Nicole |
| Andrea | Elizabeth | Juanita | Patricia |
| Angela | Frances | Julia, Julie | Paula |
| Ann, Anne | Gabriella | Katherine | Priscilla |
| Barbara | Gemma | Louise | Rita |
| Bernadette | Genevieve | Lucy | Roberta |
| Bridget | Georgia | Madeleine | Rosanne |
| Catherine | Gertrude | Marianne | Rose |
| Cecilia | Helen | Margaret | Rosemary |
| Christine | Irene | Martha | Theresa |
| Clare | Jane | Mary | Ursula |
| Colette | Jean, Jeanne | Michelle | Veronica |
| Danielle | Joan | Monica | Zita |

# Profession of Faith

"I, (Name), touching with my hand God's holy Gospels, enlightened by divine grace, profess the faith which the Catholic, Apostolic, Roman Church teaches. I believe that Church to be the one, true Church which Jesus Christ founded on earth, to which I submit with all my heart.

"I believe in God, the Father Almighty, Creator of Heaven and earth, and in Jesus Christ, His only Son, Our Lord, who was conceived by the Holy Ghost, born of the Virgin Mary, suffered under Pontius Pilate, was crucified, died and was buried. He descended into hell; the third day He arose again from the dead; He ascended into Heaven, sitteth at the right hand of God, the Father Almighty; from thence He shall come to judge the living and the dead. I believe in the Holy Ghost, the Holy Catholic Church, the Communion of Saints, the forgiveness of sins, the resurrection of the body, and life everlasting. Amen.

"I believe that seven Sacraments were instituted by Jesus Christ for the salvation of mankind: namely, Baptism, Confirmation, Holy Eucharist, Penance, Extreme Unction, Holy Orders and Matrimony.

"I believe that the Pope, the Bishop of Rome, is the Vicar of Jesus Christ on earth, that he is the supreme visible head of the whole Church and that he teaches infallibly what we must believe and do to be saved.

"I also believe everything which the Holy, Catholic, Apostolic, and Roman Church defines and declares we must believe. I adhere to her with all my heart, and I reject every error and schism which she condemns.

"So help me God and these His holy Gospels which I touch with my hand."

*Short form issued by the Holy Office, June 13, 1956.*

**175**

# How To Be A Good Catholic

1. Always attend Mass on Sundays and Holy Days, and during the week as often as possible.

2. Go to Confession every week if possible, but at least once a month.

3. Receive Holy Communion in the state of grace every time you attend Mass.

4. Be sure to receive the Sacrament of Confirmation.

5. Say your morning and evening prayers and your Rosary every day.

6. Stay away from any person, place or thing which easily leads you into sin.

7. Stay married and faithful to your spouse if you are married.

8. Accept all the children God wants to send you.

9. Raise your children to be good Catholics.

10. Devote some time every day to reading your Catholic Bible and/or sound Catholic books, to reinforce your Catholic values and the Catholic view of life.

11. Give generously to the Church and practice charity toward your neighbor.

12. Always stay in the state of grace, continually preparing for your death, remembering that death may come suddenly.

"For what shall it profit a man, if he gain the whole world, and suffer the loss of his soul? Or what shall a man give in exchange for his soul?" (Mark 8:36-37).

*If you have enjoyed this book, consider making your next selection from among the following . . .*

# —Give Copies of This Book—

*A Brief Catechism for Adults* is a brilliantly conceived and beautifully executed short, yet thorough adult catechism. Comprised of concise, clear, logically developed questions and answers, it is also supported by numerous biblical quotations before each lesson and after many answers. And, each lesson is followed by several "Practical Points," applying the principles contained in that lesson. Plus, the entire book is geared for the layman, with emphasis on the married state— since most adult lay people get married.

Thus, there is no other short catechism quite like it for brevity, charity, authoritativeness, and uncompromising adherence to the truths of the Catholic faith...There is no other book in print that is really in its class for convert instruction or adult review. And this wonderfully instructive book is needed today more so than at any other time in recent Church history.

Therefore, the Publishers are making it available at the lowest possible quantity prices for distribution to as many people as possible. Parents should order copies to give their adult children and grandparents to give their children and grandchildren. The world wastes away for want of knowledge of the Catholic faith, and *A Brief Catechism for Adults* goes a long way toward supplying that knowledge.

## Quantity Discount

|   |   |   |   |
|---|---|---|---|
| 1 copy | 12.50 | | |
| 5 copies | 9.00 each | 45.00 total | |
| 10 copies | 8.00 each | 80.00 total | |
| 25 copies | 7.00 each | 175.00 total | |
| 100 copies | 6.00 each | 600.00 total | |

### Priced low purposely for widespread distribution.

U.S. & CAN. POST/HDLG: If total order=$1-$10, add $3.00;
$10.01-$25, add $5.00; $25.01-$50, add $6.00;
$50.01-$75, add $7.00; $75.01-$150, add $8.00;
$150.01-up, add $10.00.

### At your bookdealer or direct from the Publisher.

*Prices subject to change.*

**178**